UNCONV
VEHI

ENTIONAL

CLES

Forty-Five of the Strangest Cars, Trains, Planes, Submersibles, Dirigibles, and Rockets EVER

by **MICHAEL HEARST**

illustrated by **HANS JENSSEN**

chronicle books·san francisco

TABLE O' CONTENTS

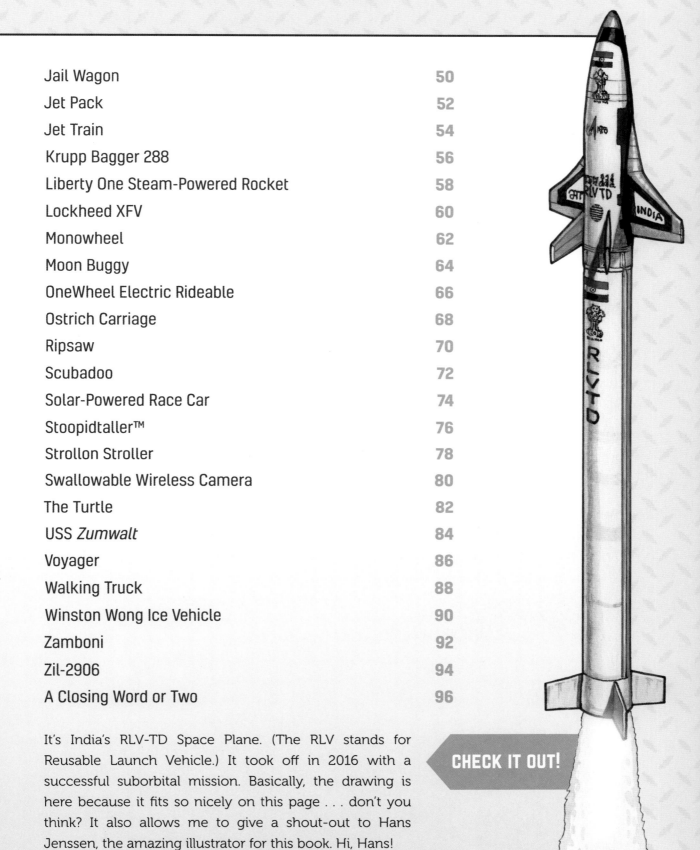

It's India's RLV-TD Space Plane. (The RLV stands for Reusable Launch Vehicle.) It took off in 2016 with a successful suborbital mission. Basically, the drawing is here because it fits so nicely on this page . . . don't you think? It also allows me to give a shout-out to Hans Jenssen, the amazing illustrator for this book. Hi, Hans!

CHECK IT OUT!

A FEW WORDS FROM MICHAEL

Hey, thanks for reading this intro! Most people skip the intro, so I'm *really* glad you're here. While I have you, here's a question: What do *you* think of when you hear the word "vehicle"? Probably a car, right? Yep, a car is definitely a vehicle. But did you know that boats, airplanes, blimps, submarines, bicycles, roller skates, and even grocery carts are vehicles? As far as I'm concerned, just about anything that moves (and typically carries something else) can be considered a vehicle. Including animals! Of course, I'm not a dictionary. I'm just a dude who likes vehicles. Especially unusual, extraordinary, curious, and UNCONVENTIONAL vehicles! BTW, tortilla chips are a type of vehicle, too! They're a vehicle for salsa (or cheese dip, if you prefer). And a pencil can be a vehicle for your clever ideas. Here, however, I'm thinking we should probably stick with more mechanical-ish things, otherwise we'll get way out of hand. Though, I kind of like it when things get a wee bit out of hand. This intro is starting to get out of hand. Okay, I'll stop now.

P.S. Look! I'm inside a 1950's Isetta three-wheeled bubble car! Please don't park in front of me or I'll never get out the door.

There are SO many kinds of vehicles out there! How about we make a list? An *official* list. (Of course, it's only official because it's in this book. Which doesn't *really* make it official at all.)

Official List

- Aerocycle
- Airplane
- Airship
- All-Terrain Vehicle
- Amphibious Vehicle
- Balloon
- Bathyscaphe
- Bicycle
- Blimp
- Boat
- Buggy
- Bulldozer
- Bus
- Cable Car
- Canoe
- Dandy Horse
- Digger
- Dirigible
- Dogsled
- Drone
- Elevator
- Excavator
- Fixed-Wing Aircraft
- Funicular
- Golf Cart
- Ground-Effect Vehicle
- Handcar

- Hang Glider
- Helicopter
- Horse-Drawn Wagon
- Hovercraft
- Hydrofoil
- Hyperloop
- Ice Skates
- Jet Pack
- Jet Ski
- Kick Scooter
- Monorail
- Monowheel
- Moped
- Motorboat
- Motorcycle
- Ornithopter
- Paddleboat
- Pogo Stick
- Quadracycle
- Rickshaw
- Rocket
- Rocket Train
- Roller Skates
- Rover
- Screw-Propelled Vehicle
- Segway
- Ship

- Short Bus
- Sled
- Spacecraft
- Stroller
- Submarine
- Submersible
- Surfboard
- Tank
- Tiltrotor Aircraft
- Tractor
- Train
- Tram
- Trencher
- Tricycle
- Truck
- Tunnel-Boring Machine
- Unicycle
- Van
- Wheelbarrow
- Wheelchair
- Yacht
- Zip Line
- _____
- _____
- _____
- _____
- _____

Can you think of some other types of vehicles? I've left a few extra spaces for you. (Wait, you may not want to actually write in this book. I mean it's fine by me if you do. But you might not. Your call.)

AIRBOARD™ PERSONAL HOVERCRAFT

MANUFACTURER: Arbortech   **DATE OF PRODUCTION:** 2000–2007

Once upon a time, the personal hovercraft was advertised in the back of comic books. But was it real? Errr . . .

It wasn't until the opening ceremony for the 2000 Summer Olympics in Sydney, Australia, that it finally showed its face. Millions of viewers were captivated. There it is! The personal hovercraft! To be specific, it was the Airboard™ Personal Hovercraft. Fill it up with gas, hop on board, and hover 8 inches (20 centimetres) above the streets, cruising at speeds up to 15 miles (24 kilometres) per hour. Sweet! Simply shift your weight to turn (which you'll need to do to avoid large puddles, sand, and other non-solid surfaces that the Airboard's motor can't handle). And wait, it runs out of gas in just one hour? Sorry, I can't hear you over all the noise this thing is making. Um, does the price tag really say $14,000? Oy.

STILL WANT ONE?

I certainly won't stop you. You can occasionally find used Airboards™ for sale on eBay for as little at $2,900. Free local pickup included!

ODE TO THE AIRBOARD

Hover here, hover there.
Hover in your underwear.
You can hover down the street
(but only if the street's concrete).
The four-stroke engine loudly roars.
Sorry, Mom, no time for chores—
I'm lifting up! I'm moving free.
But why is everyone looking at me?
Are they mesmerized by my hover stance?
Or is it because I have no pants?

As seen in the back of comic books from the 1960s and '70s. Well, sort of. The ad asked you to send $3.50 for plans and a photo. Awesome! Yes, I was that kid in the '70s who sent off his allowance money for hovercraft plans. And yes, I'm still waiting for them to arrive.

7

AIRBUS BELUGA

MANUFACTURER: Airbus   **DATE OF PRODUCTION:** 1992–1999

"Bulbous" is the word that comes to mind when I look at this airplane. The A300-600ST Super Transporter, more commonly referred to as the Airbus Beluga, is used to carry airplane parts—*big* airplane parts—from one Airbus assembly location in Europe to another. We're talking entire fuselages, wings, and tails, all loaded into the upper deck of the airplane through its massive forehead. Five of these planes have been flying around since the 1990s, but what will they do when airplanes get even bigger? I guess they'll need to build an even bigger Beluga. Oh, wait, they are! Coming soon: the Beluga XL.

OPEN WIDE

Although the Airbus Beluga is a variation on the standard A300 airliner, which can seat 266 passengers, this cargo plane flies with just two pilots and an engineer. The rest of the 184-foot (56-metre) beast is simply a gigantic carrying case. In addition to hauling Airbus parts, the Beluga has also been chartered to transport relief supplies, entire helicopters, modules for NASA, and even, once, an oversized painting from the Louvre.

BELUGA WHALE VERSUS BELUGA AIRPLANE

• An adult beluga whale weighs 3,000 pounds (1,400 kilograms) on average. A Beluga airplane weighs 191,000 pounds (86,600 kilograms).

• A beluga whale can swim backward. A Beluga airplane cannot. (Move backward, I mean. It can't swim in any direction.) A pushback tractor is used to move the airplane in reverse.

• The beluga whale's forehead changes shape when it makes sounds. The shape of the Airbus Beluga's head does not change shape (unless you consider opening the cargo door).

• Beluga whales eat up to 60 pounds (27 kilograms) of food a day. The Airbus Beluga consumes up to 9,095 U.S. gallons (269 litres) of fuel in a single flight.

• The Beluga whale is threatened by oil and gas development. The Airbus Beluga is threatened by a *lack* of oil and gas development.

AIRFISH 8

MANUFACTURER: Wigetworks   **DATE OF PRODUCTION:** 2010

Nope, it's not taking off. And no, it's not landing. The cruising altitude for the Airfish 8 is only up to 23 feet (7 metres) above water. Technically, it's not an airplane at all (or a boat or hovercraft, for that matter). It's a ground-effect vehicle—a hybrid that uses what's known as the "ground effect" to glide just a few feet above the waves. Powered by only a V8 car engine, the Airfish 8 can carry 8 to 10 passengers and travel up to 122 miles (196 kilometres) per hour (three times faster than most cruiser-style motorboats). Although it's still being tested, Wigetworks hopes the Airfish will soon be used for tourism, sea patrol, and just about any marine travel you can think of. In other words, they hope it *takes off*. (See what I did there?)

WHAT IS THIS "GROUND EFFECT" YOU SPEAK OF?

In short, ground effect is when the airflow beneath the wings is interrupted by the surface underneath it (the ground, for instance, or water, as in this case). The interruption creates additional lift and less drag. Don't believe me? Ask just about any large bird.

HOW DO YOU SAY, "BEEN THERE, DONE THAT" IN RUSSIAN?

Bartini Beriev VVA-14 (1972)

This Cold War creature was designed to fly as both a ground-effect vehicle and a high-altitude aircraft. The VVA-14 was built in response to the threat of American missile submarines. It made 107 flights before retiring to the Russian Air Force Museum.

Lun Ekranoplan MD-160 (1987)

Powered by eight massive jet engines, this Ekranpolan (or "screen plane") still holds the record for greatest lift for any aircraft. We're talking 1,000 tons (910 metric tons) of lift! (That's the ability to lift 1,000 tons, including itself.) The MD-160 could travel at 300 miles (483 kilometres) per hour just 13 feet (4 metres) above the water while carrying 1,000 soviet marines. Although the Ekranoplan is no longer in service, Russia continues to work on new and improved versions of it.

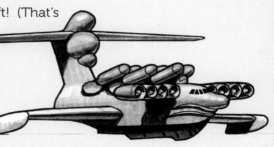

AUTOALVEARE

MANUFACTURER: Lancia Industrial Vehicles   **DATE OF PRODUCTION:** 1930–1932

Double-decker buses are super cool. Triple-decker buses are even cooler! (And sort of a bad idea.) As you can probably guess, they aren't exactly a "stable" concept. Take a turn too fast, and flipty-doo. Not to mention the problems of low-hanging trees, stoplights, and overpasses. Nonetheless, in the 1930s, Lancia built the Autoalveare for travel between Rome and Tivoli, Italy. The Italian word "alveare" translates to "hive," as in beehive. Many bees can squeeze into one beehive. Similarly, many passengers could squeeze into one Autoalveare. (Hopefully, no bees entered the bus.) According to an old issue of *Popular Mechanics*, the bus had enough room for 85 passengers as well as a smoking compartment, room for dogs, and could handle 440 pounds (200 kilograms) of baggage. Thankfully, there are no reports of the bus (or the dogs, or the smokers) ever tipping over. Perhaps because the bus moved at just 28 miles (45 kilometres) per hour.

TRIPLE-DECKER? (I MEAN, SORT OF.)

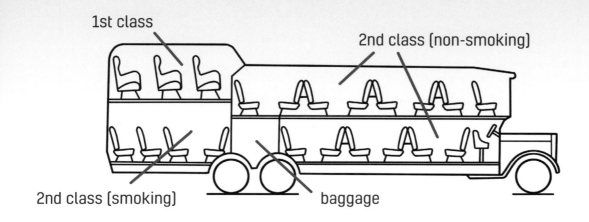

1st class

2nd class (non-smoking)

2nd class (smoking)

baggage

WHAT ABOUT THE "KNIGHT BUS" FROM HARRY POTTER?

KNIGHT BUS

It's true, a triple-decker bus was built for the filming of *Harry Potter and the Prisoner of Azkaban*. And it really worked (minus the high-speed zipping, stretching, and disappearing)! Replicas of the vehicle are on display at the Warner Bros. Studio Tour in London and at Universal Studios in Orlando, Florida.

BATHYSCAPHE *TRIESTE*

MANUFACTURER: Auguste Piccard   **DATE OF PRODUCTION:** 1953

Did you know that the deepest-known location in ALL the oceans is called Challenger Deep (named after the ship that discovered it, the HMS *Challenger*)? It's part of the Mariana Trench, found in the Pacific Ocean, southwest of Guam, and it's an insane 35,000+ feet (10,000+ metres) below the surface of the sea. That's the distance of more than 24 Empire State Buildings stacked on top of each other! Until 1960, no human or vehicle had ever visited Challenger Deep due to the super-intense water pressure at such depths. That is, until Bathyscaphe *Trieste* was built. Designed by a Swiss scientist, constructed in Italy, and then purchased by the U.S. Navy, the vehicle was similar to a rigid balloon (see page 36); however, instead of being filled with air or gas, it was filled with gasoline (for buoyancy, not fuel). The cabin underneath had steel walls that were 7 inches (18 centimetres) thick, protecting two men on a nearly five-hour descent to Challenger Deep, where the pressure was 8 tons per square inch (1,125 kilograms per square centimetre)! As you can imagine, the ride was not easy—the temperature inside the cabin dropped to 45 degrees Fahrenheit (7 degrees Celsius), and when the bathyscaphe reached a depth of 30,000 feet (9,000 metres), one of the outer windows cracked, dramatically shuddering the entire vessel. The pilots, realizing they were still alive, decided to continue their mission. Yikes!

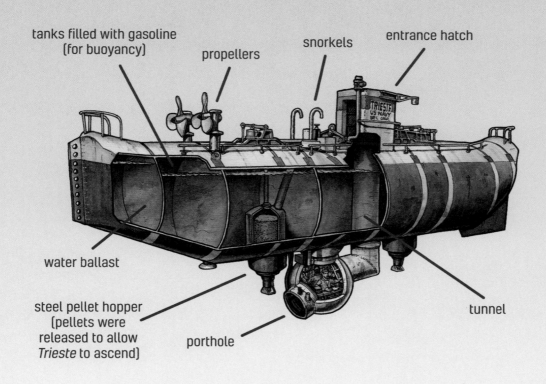

tanks filled with gasoline
(for buoyancy)

propellers

snorkels

entrance hatch

water ballast

steel pellet hopper
(pellets were
released to allow
Trieste to ascend)

porthole

tunnel

INCIDENTALLY

Challenger Deep has been visited several more times over the years—twice by unmanned vehicles, and in 2012 by a submersible called *Deepsea Challenger* (piloted by Canadian filmmaker James Cameron).

IN CASE YOU'RE WONDERING

"Bathy" means "deep." "Scaphe" means "vessel." A "bathyscaphe" (pronounced bath-a-skaf) is a self-propelled vehicle used for deep-sea dives. It can dive much deeper than a submarine. And unlike a bathy**sphere** (which is usually tethered to a ship), the bathy**scaphe** can dive freely. I'm sure it would be interesting to ride in a bathyscaphe, but I would much prefer to es*caf* to a warm bath.

BEER BIKE

MANUFACTURER: Het Fietscafe BV   **DATE OF PRODUCTION:** 1997–present

*J*ah jah, hier kommt das Bier Bike! Nothing says "party" (or perhaps "tourist") quite like a bicycle built for sixteen, pedaling through the center of town . . . with a keg of beer on the front! This human-powered Dr. Seuss-esque vehicle was first introduced by the Dutch company Het Fiestcafe (which translates to "bicycle café"). According to sources, the bike was invented by brothers Henk and Zwier Van Laar, who wanted to help promote their local pub in a parade. It was such a hit that they began renting out the bike, and soon the idea caught on in other parts of the world—especially in beer-loving Germany. Although beer bikes vary, there's typically room for 10 to 17 people, including several non-pedaling free-loaders, a bartender, and one designated driver. *G'suffa!*

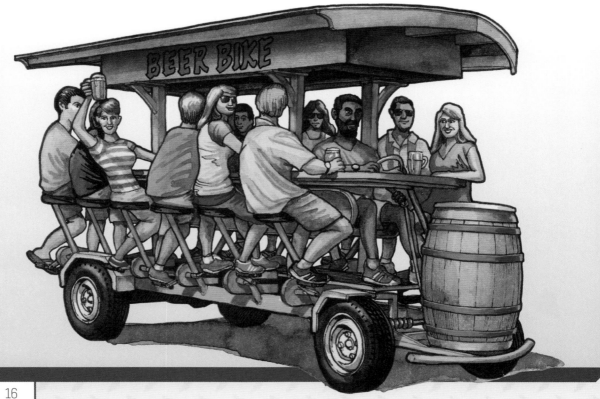

BEER-WHEEL DRIVE

"Bike" is short for "bicycle." The "bi" in "bicycle" refers to two wheels. This thing, however, has four wheels. Shouldn't it be a Beer Quadricycle? I suppose Beer Bike sounds better. On that note, this vehicle is also known as a "party bike," "pedal crawler," "cycle pub," and about 20 other names. What would you call it?

BEER BIKE BAN

In 2017, Amsterdam banned beer bikes from the center of the Dutch city. About 6,000 locals signed a petition, calling on the council to outlaw the vehicles, referring to them as a "terrible phenomenon."

LEARNING GERMAN IS EASY AND FUN!

ja ("yah") – – – – – – – – – yes

hier ("heer") – – – – – – – – here

kommt ("kumpt") – – – – – – comes

das ("doss") – – – – – – – – the

bier ("beer") – – – – – – – – beer

bike ("bike") – – – – – – – – bike

g'suffa ("gzoo-fah") – – – – – – drink up!

NOTE: There are many other words in the German language. However, this should get you started.

BELL X-1

MANUFACTURER: Bell Aircraft   **DATE OF PRODUCTION:** 1945

Perhaps you already know that the Bell X-1 (piloted by Charles E. "Chuck" Yeager) was the first manned airplane to travel faster than the speed of sound. But did you know it was powered by a four-chambered rocket engine? And did you know that it never took off from a runway on its own? Instead, it was dropped from a modified B29 bomber at an altitude of over 20,000 feet (6,000 metres)! Yeager had to climb down a ladder from the belly of the B-29 into the X-1's cockpit. He would then strap on his oxygen mask while the cockpit door lowered to seal him in. With the yank of a lever, the X-1 would free-fall (just like the bombs the B29 was meant to drop) until the rocket engine ignited, thrusting the X-1 to a record-breaking speed of 957 miles (1,500 kilometres) per hour. *Whooooooooosh!!!* Only after all the fuel had been burned (or jettisoned, as was often the case) would the X-1 be light enough to glide to a landing—while typically still traveling at speeds of nearly 200 miles (320 kilometres) per hour. That's not an easy landing to stick.

SONIC BOOM!

No, we're not talking about that blue hedgehog. We're referring to the loud booming noise associated with shock waves created when an airplane moves faster than the speed of sound—around 767 miles (1,234 kilometres) per hour, to be precise (otherwise known as Mach 1). On October 14, 1947, with Chuck Yeager at its controls, the X-1 made the world's first supersonic flight!

TRUE OR TRUE?

1. Chuck Yeager had two busted ribs (from falling off a horse) the day he broke the sound barrier!

2. Many people thought an airplane could never go faster than the speed of sound because the shock wave would destroy the airplane.

3. As the X-1 approached the speed of sound, it lost the ability to be controlled. As soon as the sound barrier was broken, however, the plane stabilized.

4. The B29, which dropped the X-1, is also the same type of plane that unfortunately dropped some pretty terrible bombs on Japan a few years earlier.

5. The cracking sound you hear from a whip being snapped is actually a mini sonic boom. The tip of the whip is moving more than 767 miles (1,234 kilometres) per hour!

6. The X-1 is now in the Smithsonian Institution in Washington, D.C. You should go see it!

Answers: 1. True 2. True 3. True 4. True 5. True 6. True

BERTHA: TUNNEL-BORING MACHINE

MANUFACTURER: Hitachi Zosen Sakai Works   **DATE OF PRODUCTION:** 2013

She did it! Bertha drilled her way under downtown Seattle, leaving behind a whopping 57-foot-wide, 1.7-mile-long (17-metre-wide, 2.7-kilometre-long) paved tunnel! Moving at an average speed of 35 feet (11 metre) per day—a snail can move up to 82 feet (25 metres) in a day—it took her almost four years to complete the journey. Of course, things don't always go as planned, like the time Bertha ran into an old pipe, which jammed her up and caused her to overheat, ultimately setting the entire project back by two years! Oops. But still, *she persisted.* Bertha, the largest tunnel-boring machine (TBM) ever built, broke through to daylight on April 4, 2017. Sadly, soon after, Bertha was disassembled into hundreds of smaller pieces, many of which were sold for parts. (*Sniff.*) On a positive note, much of her steel has been reused in the making of the tunnel, allowing her tremendous strength to live on. Go Bertha!

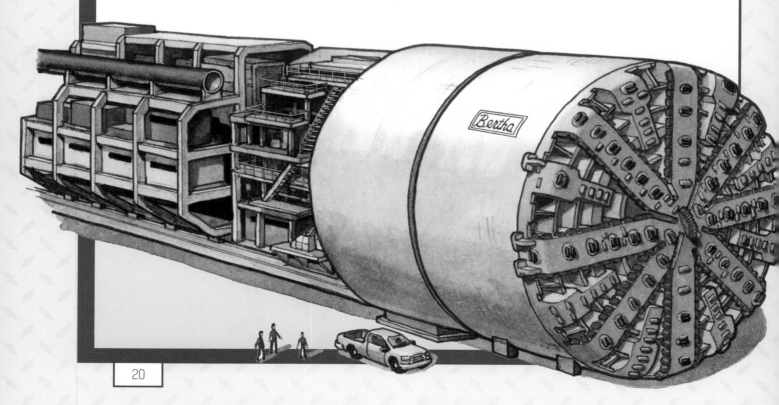

THE BIRTH OF BERTHA (and other fun facts)

• Bertha was built for the Washington State Department of Transportation by the Hitachi Zosen company in Japan for $80 million.

• Bertha was the world's largest tunnel-boring machine at 326 feet (99 metres) long and weighing 6,700 tons (6,100 metric tons). An average of 25 people operated Bertha at any one time.

• Inside the enormous machine were catwalks, ladders, stairs, a control room, and several break rooms.

• The tunnel was dug to replace a stretch of highway (the Alaskan Way Viaduct), which was heavily damaged in a 2001 earthquake.

• Bertha was named after Seattle's first female mayor, Bertha Knight Landes, a remarkable woman who also persisted to get some big jobs done.

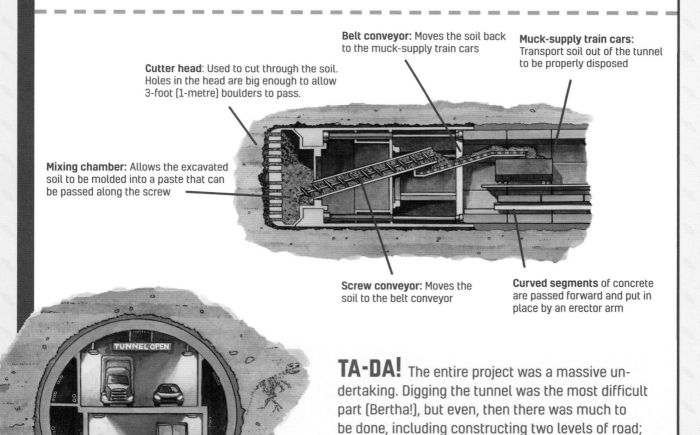

Belt conveyor: Moves the soil back to the muck-supply train cars

Muck-supply train cars: Transport soil out of the tunnel to be properly disposed

Cutter head: Used to cut through the soil. Holes in the head are big enough to allow 3-foot (1-metre) boulders to pass.

Mixing chamber: Allows the excavated soil to be molded into a paste that can be passed along the screw

Screw conveyor: Moves the soil to the belt conveyor

Curved segments of concrete are passed forward and put in place by an erector arm

TA-DA! The entire project was a massive undertaking. Digging the tunnel was the most difficult part (Bertha!), but even, then there was much to be done, including constructing two levels of road; installing vents, emergency exits, lighting, and fire-detection systems; and conducting a zillion safety tests.

BIG WIND

MANUFACTURER: MB Drilling   **DATE OF PRODUCTION:** 1991

Sometimes it takes a recycled T-34 tank with a couple of MiG 21 fighter jet engines to put out a fire. Really BIG fires! Like the burning oil fields in Kuwait after the Gulf War. Operated by three people (a driver, a fire chief, and a controller in the back), it blasts water from six nozzles into the exhaust of the two jet engines, which are directed toward the inferno. We're talking 220 gallons (833 litres) of water per second into jet engine exhaust that's blowing up to 770 miles (1,240 kilometres) per hour. Brilliantly, a Hungarian team was able to pull this vehicle together to take care of what no other firefighting machine could handle. I'm thinking I may use Big Wind to blow out the candles at my next birthday party. Or would that be overkill?

T-34 heavy tank

**Mikoyan-Gurevich
MiG 21 fighter jet**

A T-34 tank with the gun turret removed plus two MiG 21 jet engines equals Big Wind! About 220 gallons (833 litres) of water a second (far more than most U.S. houses use in 24 hours) are pumped through the six nozzles and sprayed into the jet exhaust, creating one seriously fierce blast of steam.

BIG WATER

BIG WIND

BIG FIRE!

BIG WIND, LITTLE POEM

It takes a big wind to tame a big fire.
If you call upon this beast,
we hope your needs are dire.
Of course, you'll need some water handy,
lest you look a fool—
for the Big Wind, in under a minute,
can drain an entire pool.

DOMICOPTER

MANUFACTURER: Tom Hatton, Aerosight, and Domino's Pizza, Inc. **DATE OF PRODUCTION:** 2013

Thank you for reading my book. I'm rewarding you with a Domino's Meat Lovers Pizza, delivered by drone. It'll be there any minute now.

We all know drones (also known as unmanned aerial vehicles, or UAVs) are used for recreational flying as well as aerial surveillance. But why not use them to deliver pizzas? Well, because the FAA* and CAA** won't allow it, for one. But that didn't stop Tom Hatton from the UK-based creative agency T + Biscuits from approaching Domino's Pizza with this clever idea for the DomiCopter! He enlisted Dean Wynton of Aerosight to build and pilot the modified CarbonCore Octocopter for a little promotional video . . . a video that got picked up by NBC News, the *Tonight Show,* Fox News, the *HuffPost,* and just about every other news source you can think of. With over a million views on YouTube in just 10 days, the campaign proved to be a rather astonishing publicity stunt at a time when Domino's Pizza's social media presence was flopping. Although the DomiCopter never actually went into production, this one-of-a-kind vehicle certainly did its job in attracting attention. Hopefully Tom and Dean were rewarded with Meat Lovers Pizzas.

*Federal Aviation Administration
**Civil Aeronautics Authority

NOT TO DRONE ON, BUT . . .

Unmanned aerial vehicles have been around for quite some time. You can even look back at 1849, when Austria used bomb-filled balloons to attack Italy (which is pretty much the opposite of pizza delivery).

HEAD SPINNING?

The DomiCopter is a "multicopter" drone—to be specific, an octocopter with eight propellers. Piloted with a remote control on the ground, the rotors can turn in either direction and at various speeds, allowing the vehicle to move up, down, left, right, forward, and backward.

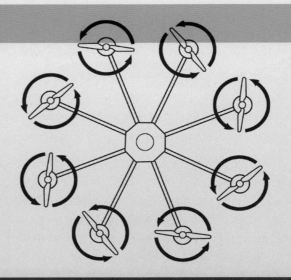

E-SHIP 1

MANUFACTURER: Lindenau Werft and Cassens-Werft   **DATE OF PRODUCTION:** 2008

Ever heard of the Magnus effect? That's okay, neither had I. It's a phenomenon! Basically, if you take a cylinder and rotate it fast enough, it forces air to move across one side more quickly than the other. Spin a large enough cylinder (or perhaps four of them), and it might just propel a vehicle. Yep, those 88-foot- (27-metre-) tall columns on the E-Ship 1 are known as Flettner rotors, and their spinning provides most of the ship's propulsion! There's also a standard rotor propeller on the back of the ship, but the Flettner rotors cut down significantly on fuel consumption and pollution . . . a good thing for a world of much-needed sustainable/green transportation. BTW, did I mention that the purpose of this ship is to transport wind turbines? High five (or four) to the E-Ship 1.

WAIT, WHAT??

The rotor spins, causing the air to flow faster on one side than the other. Because of the Magnus effect, the ship is "pulled" toward the side with faster moving air, where the air pressure is lower. The direction and speed of the rotor's rotation can be adjusted to meet wind conditions. Similar to sails on a sailboat, the rotors are useless without sufficient wind.

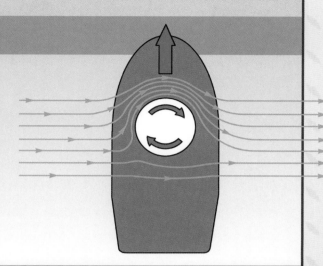

MINISCULE GLOSSARY OF POTENTIAL USEFULNESS

Heinrich Gustav Magnus (1802–1870): As you may have guessed, the Magnus effect was named after a German physicist who wrote about the effect in 1852. However, Sir Isaac Newton had actually described the phenomenon nearly 200 years earlier. So why is it not called the Newton effect? Oh, well.

Anton Flettner (1885–1961): An aviation engineer, who, along with Albert Betz, Jacob Ackeret, Ludwig Prandtl, and Albert Einstein, built the Buckau—the first rotor ship, in 1924. Flettner rotors have also been used on various aircraft.

Curveball: In baseball, the Magnus effect is the reason a curveball travels out of its straight path. The ball spins, and thus curves toward the side with faster-moving air. This can also be applied to other ball sports, like soccer, table tennis, and golf . . . though you might wish to avoid it in golf.

NOT SO NEW

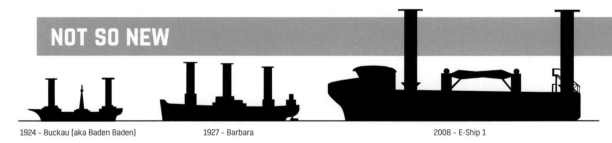

1924 - Buckau (aka Baden Baden)   1927 - Barbara   2008 - E-Ship 1

Other ships with Flettner rotors have existed previously, but it wasn't until recently that materials finally advanced enough to make production cost-efficient. Time to make it happen for real, yo!

ELEMMENT PALAZZO

MANUFACTURER: Marchi Mobile **DATE OF PRODUCTION:** 2013-present

This is one seriously fancy motor home . . . with the word "home" being an understatement. Designed by Luigi Colania, a famous German industrial designer, this beast is really more like a motor *mansion*. With up to 732 square feet (68 square metres) of interior space, the RV is built around a Volvo 600-horsepower (447-kilowatt) turbocharge diesel engine. In case the 13-foot (4-metre) lounge sofa within reach of the bar and the British royal king-size bed aren't enough, there's a self-cleaning toilet, towel dryer, and therapeutic rain shower. If those aren't enough, there are the two 42-inch (1-metre) LED screens, onboard mobile internet, and a Steinway reference audio system. If those aren't enough, well, then I suppose you can just hang out upstairs in the Sky Lounge!

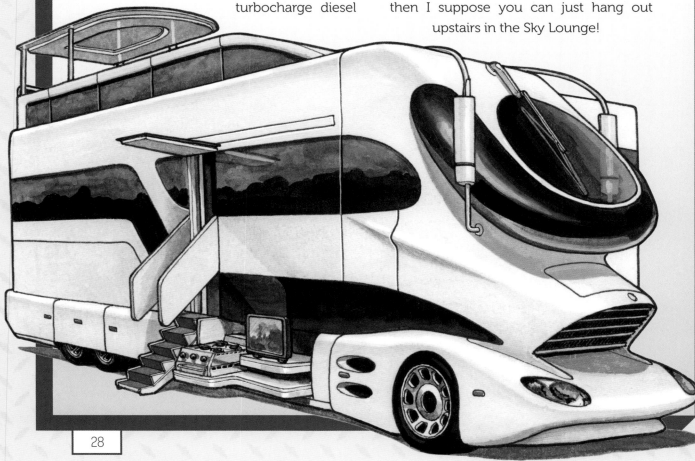

SKY LOUNGE?

With a simple press of a button, banquette seats rise from the body, and walls flip up to create an enclosed terrace and a canopy-covered roof (complete with mood lighting). It makes for one fancy hangout!

CAN I AFFORD ONE OF THESE?

The eleMMent Palazzo goes for around $3 million. Not to worry, financial services are available.

FLYING CATHEDRAL

MANUFACTURER: Kubicek Balloons   **DATE OF PRODUCTION:** 2002

Who says hot-air balloons have to be round? Certainly not Jan Kaeser or Martin Zimmermann, the artists who conceived this awesome floating tribute to the Cathedral of Saint Gall. The 101-foot (31-metre) Flying Cathedral, which consists of numerous polyester panels sewn together by Kubicek Balloons, was constructed just in time to celebrate the 200th anniversary of the canton (or state) of St. Gallen, Switzerland. Carrying a pilot and up to two passengers in its basket, the balloon flew on 45 occasions throughout Switzerland, France, Belgium, Austria, England, Japan, Germany, and the United States. But what does one do with a cathedral balloon after the celebrating is done? Well, you sell it to an art collector (or rather an *art balloon* collector) in the Dominican Republic. Fly on, cathedral!

ABBY NORMAL

Located in the town of St. Gallen, the non-balloon version of the cathedral (i.e., the *real* cathedral) was constructed between 1755 and 1766 and is part of a larger eighth-century Benedictine abbey. It is safe to say that *it* won't float away.

P.S. Yes, I stole the Abby Normal thing from one of my all-time favorite movies, *Young Frankenstein.*

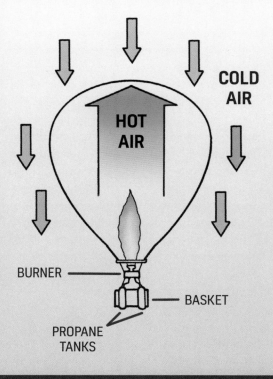

COLD AIR

HOT AIR

BURNER

BASKET

PROPANE TANKS

JUST A LOT OF HOT AIR

Hot-air balloons date back to at least the 1700s. Simply enough, the air inside the balloon is heated, making it lighter than the outside air. Perhaps you've heard someone say "hot air rises." Turns out it's true!

P.S. While the unmanned balloon bombs on page 25 were filled with hot air, the Graf Zeppelin on page 36 (which is not a balloon, but rather a rigid airship) was filled with hydrogen—a gas that's also lighter than air.

FLYING JELLYFISH

MANUFACTURER: Leif Ristroph and Stephen Childress **DATE OF PRODUCTION:** 2013

It's a bird! It's a plane! It's a miniature flying robot jellyfish! (I personally think it looks more like a moth.) To be fair, it was only *after* being built that Leif Ristroph, a mathematician at New York University, realized his invention operated somewhat like jellyfish and named it after them. Either way, this tiny robot has the remarkable ability to fly through the air and remain upright while flapping its wings. A motor at the center of the Aerojelly rotates, which cranks the arms in and out, pushing the Mylar wings up and down. And

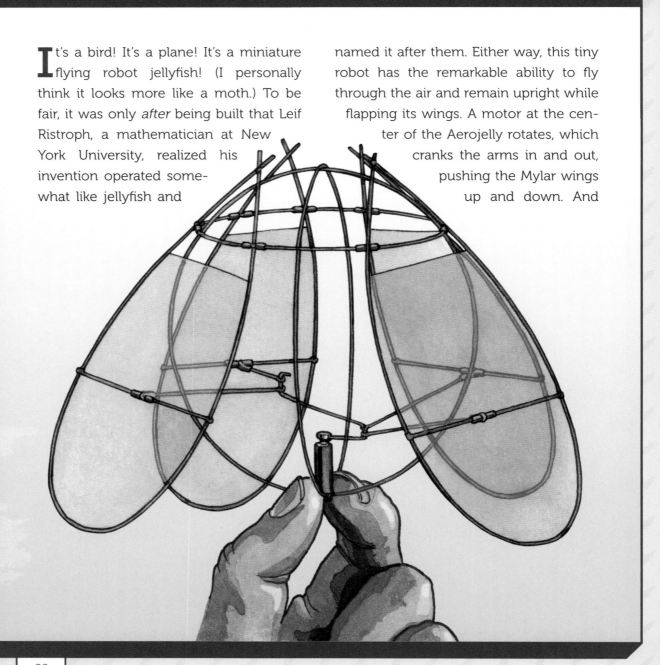

to think—the Aerojelly was made from parts purchased from hobby airplane websites for about $15! And now what? Many have suggested its use as a surveillance device (because we certainly need more of those?!), or maybe it could help with search-and-rescue missions in tight spaces? As Ristroph has stated, "I like to imagine that you make hundreds of the flyers and throw them out above New York City to test air quality and other things."

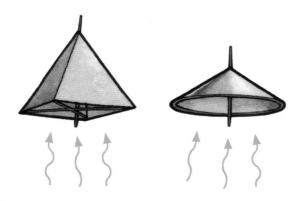

The inventors first tested small pyramids and cones to see how these basic shapes would float when hit with blasts of air.

The Aerojelly works on a similar principal to the jellyfish. The same way a jellyfish pushes water out of its bell, the Aerojelly pushes air out from its wings.

CONTRARY TO WHAT YOU MIGHT THINK . . .

. . . it's much more difficult to fly something tiny than to fly something large. And yet, this miniature **ornithopter** (a fancy word for an aircraft with flapping wings) can amazingly stay upright while moving through the air. If the Aerojelly begins to tip, the motion of the flapping wings will naturally correct its course. How cool is that?

GAS-TURBINE MOTORCYCLE

MANUFACTURER: Various **DATE OF PRODUCTION:** 2000–present

Zhiiiiiioooowwwwwww! That's the sound of a turbine engine roaring by. But it's not an airplane; it's a motorcycle! Yep, a motorcycle with a turbine engine, which can reach speeds of well over 200 miles (322 kilometres) per hour. There are several gas-turbine land-racing motorcycles out there, including the Y2K Superbike, built by Marine Turbine Technologies (one of which sits in Jay Leno's garage). However, as a fan of the underdog, my personal favorite is the JU-01 (or Johansson Unit 01), hand-built in 2010 by Swedish hobbyist Anders Johansson. Despite the lack of sponsorship (as well as the parts being milled, welded, and cast in his own workshop), Anders has taken his turbine bike to a speed of 190 miles (306 kilometres) per hour. Not too shabby! He's currently working on a new engine, which he hopes will have nearly double the horsepower and will stand a chance to break the land-speed record for this class of motorcycle—a title administered by the Southern California Timing Association and currently held by Paul Thede, at 215.96 miles (347.55 kilometres) per hour. Once again, I say, *Zhiiiiiioooowwwwwww!*

JET ENGINE?

JET ENGINE

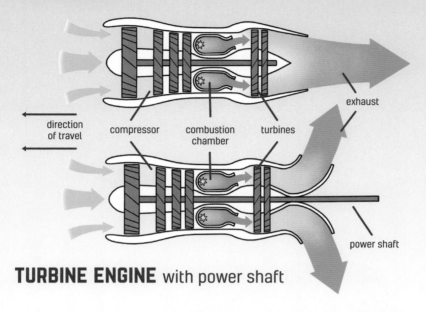

direction
of travel

compressor

combustion
chamber

turbines

exhaust

power shaft

TURBINE ENGINE with power shaft

Not exactly. A turbine engine on a jet airplane uses its exhaust or **thrust** to move the airplane forward. With a turbine motorcycle, the engine's output turns a power shaft, which then turns the rear wheel. Many helicopters and other aircraft (see page 52) work in a similar manner.

The current land-speed record for ANY motorcycle is a whopping 376 miles (605 kilometres) per hour, set in 2010 by the Ack Attack streamline motorcycle. It uses twin Suzuki engines (not turbine engines) and looks more like a sideways two-wheeled rocket.

DID YOU KNOW?

Turbine motorcycles are street-legal! But if you're in a car, you might not want to tailgate a gas-turbine motorcycle . . . unless you want your front bumper to melt off.

GRAF ZEPPELIN AIRSHIP

MANUFACTURER: Luftschiffbau Zeppelin Company **DATE OF PRODUCTION:** 1926–1928

Did you know that 10 years before the first commercial airplane carr-ied passengers across the Atlantic Ocean, you could travel from Germany to the United States and back aboard a 776-foot-(237-metre)-long, hydrogen-filled "rigid airship"? Behold, the LZ 127 Graf Zeppelin! In just four days (three days on the return trip), 20 passengers (along with 40 crew members) could travel from Friedrichshafen, Germany, to Lakehurst, New Jersey, cruising at an average speed of 72 miles (116 kilometres) per hour, approximately 650 feet (198 metres) above the ocean. Throughout its nine-year career, the LZ 127 made 590 flights, carrying 34,000 passengers in total. Amazingly, the only near-disaster took place on its maiden voyage across the Atlantic in 1928, when it hit a storm near Bermuda, which tore off a large portion of the tail-fin covering. Thankfully (and amazingly), the crew was able to repair it in-flight! The same can't be said for the LZ 129 (aka Hindenburg), which caught fire in 1937 while attempting to dock in New Jersey, killing 36 people, and putting an end to the golden age of airships.

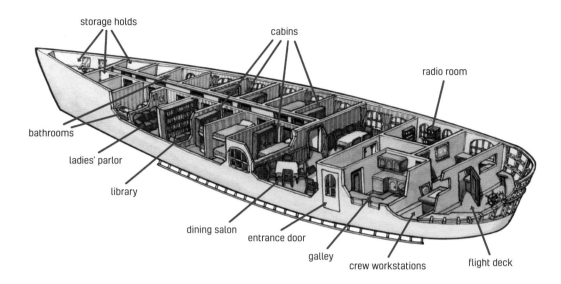

storage holds

cabins

radio room

bathrooms

ladies' parlor

library

dining salon

entrance door

galley

crew workstations

flight deck

Most of the Graf Zeppelin was filled with hydrogen to provide lift. Passengers were contained in the much smaller gondola, which hung from the bottom front of the ship.

First of all, both zeppelins and blimps are airships or dirigibles. The word "dirigible" really just means "steerable." A balloon cannot be steered, however, so it is not a dirigible. That said, a blimp is more like a balloon in structure, but with fins and an engine. A zeppelin, on the other hand, has a hard frame or skeleton. Does that make sense? I didn't think so.

Did I mention the LZ 127 was 776 feet (237 metres) long? That's more than three times the length of a Boeing 747!

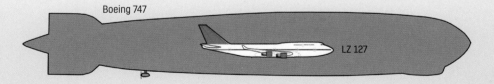

Boeing 747

LZ 127

HAMMETSCHWAND ELEVATOR

MANUFACTURER: Wüest & Co. AG   **DATE OF PRODUCTION:** 1903–1905

Are *you* brave enough to ride this sketchy-looking outdoor elevator? When first built in 1905 by the nearby Bürgenstock Hotel, it was made out of wood and sheet metal. *Gulp!* Seven people at a time would cram into the cab and ride 500 feet (153 metres) to the top of the Bürgenstock Plateau, a breathtaking 3,714 feet (1,132 metres) above sea level, where they would take in scenic views of Lake Lucerne and the Swiss Alps. Thankfully, the elevator has since been refurbished with much sturdier metal and glass. Though, I'm not sure that really helps if you suffer from vertigo, and the elevator just happens to get stuck . . .

46 + 454 = 500 (14 + 139 = 153)

The first 46 feet (14 metres) of the ascent are inside the mountain and along the cliff face. The elevator then travels another 454 feet (139 metres) through open air until it reaches the top of the lattice tower, where you can walk (or flee) across a narrow bridge to the vantage point.

INCIDENTALLY

In 1935, after receiving a speed upgrade from 3.3 feet (1 metre) per second to almost 9 feet (3 metres) per second, the Hammetschwand Elevator was the fastest in the world. That record has since been broken (some elevators now move more than 50 feet [15 metres] per second!); however, it still remains the highest outdoor elevator in Europe.

GOING DOWN?

In case you're curious (and I know you are), the world's tallest elevator is at AngloGold Ashanti Mponeng Gold Mine in South Africa. The entire ride is 7,490 feet (2,283 metres) into the ground, which is almost three times the height of the world's tallest building!

HANDCAR

MANUFACTURER: Various   **DATE OF PRODUCTION:** c. 1880–1910

How about *this* clunky monkey! In the train world, the handcar is a small rail car powered by its passengers—in other words, human power! Used for track maintenance and inspections, these vehicles were sort of like the pickup truck of the late 1800s and early 1900s. There have been many variations of the railway handcar—my personal favorite being the cartoonish pump car, based on a patent by George S. Sheffield in 1883. The pump car was powered by one or more people using nothing more than elbow grease to move the seesaw lever up and down, which turned a single gear and propelled the car forward. Here I should mention that a typical handcar weighed 500 to 600 pounds (230 to 270 kilograms) and carried up to 12 workers along a designated stretch of track 4 to 12 miles (6 to 19 kilo-

metres) long, cruising at an average speed of 8 miles (13 kilometres) per hour—not exactly the bullet train of Japan (see page 55). Things were a little easier when traveling downhill . . . that is, until they hit an extra-steep grade. Thankfully, the handcar also had a foot-pedal brake. Additionally, should an express train appear on the horizon, the entire handcar could be lifted and removed from the track. All of this sounds like a lower-back problem to me.

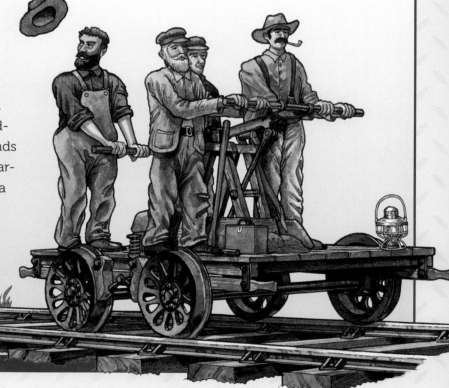

DID YOU SAY TWELVE WORKERS?

Why, yes, I did. Known as a section gang, there are reports of up to 12 workers squeeeeeeezing onto a single handcar. In all fairness, however, a gang was typically just 4 to 6 people . . . plus their tools.

WHAT SORTS OF TOOLS ARE YOU TALKING ABOUT?

You know, things like shovels, hammers, chisels, rail benders, spike-removal claws, and just about anything else you can think of to fix a track.

FACE FORWARD!

Despite cartoons and movies showing two guys facing each other on the handcar, it was common practice (and much safer) for everyone to face forward.

HELIOS SOLAR AIRCRAFT

MANUFACTURER: AeroVironment **DATE OF PRODUCTION:** 1999

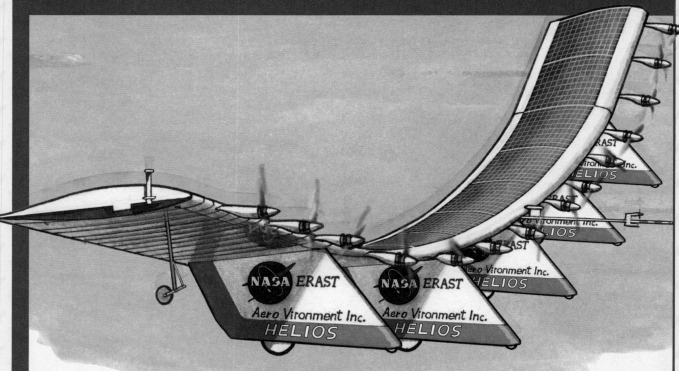

Who needs fuel when we've got the sun? The Helios Protoype was the fourth and final (and coolest-looking) unmanned solar aircraft developed by NASA between 1983 and 2003. The idea was simple: Prove that solar-electric-powered, high-altitude aircrafts were possible. Not only did the Helios prove exactly that, but in 2001 it also set the record for highest unmanned aircraft. We're talking 96,863 feet (29,524 metres) above sea level (more than twice the height of most commercial airplanes)! Unfortunately, in 2003 the Helios had a somewhat less successful flight. High winds and turbulence caused the delicate wing to flex more than it could handle, and the Helios broke apart and fell into the Pacific Ocean. Oh well, it was fun while it lasted.

FIVE FUN FLYING FACTS

1. An aircraft that looks like one big wing is typically called a flying wing. Imagine that.

2. The word "aircraft" is different from "airplane." An aircraft is any machine that can fly. An airplane is an aircraft with fixed wings. The Helios does *not* have fixed wings. It *is* a wing!

3. The wingspan of the Helios Prototype is 247 feet (75 metres), which is nearly the length of a football field.

4. Takeoff and landing speed for the Helios is about the same as the average cruising speed of a bicycle.

5. The higher you go into the atmosphere, the more intense the sunlight—which means more power for a solar-powered aircraft!

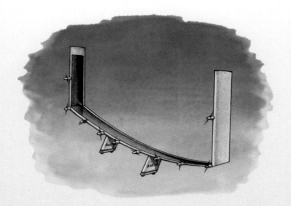

INCIDENTALLY (#1)

In 2014, Boeing patented a solar-powered unmanned airplane they believe can fly "forever" and can be used in a similar manner as communication satellites. We shall see.

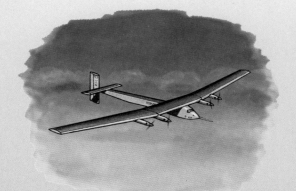

INCIDENTALLY (#2)

There have been other successful solar aircrafts and airplanes, perhaps most famously the Solar Impulse 2, which completed the first round-the-world trip in 2016 . . . with a pilot!

HUMAN CANNONBALL TRUCK

MANUFACTURER: Various **DATE OF PRODUCTION:** 1930s

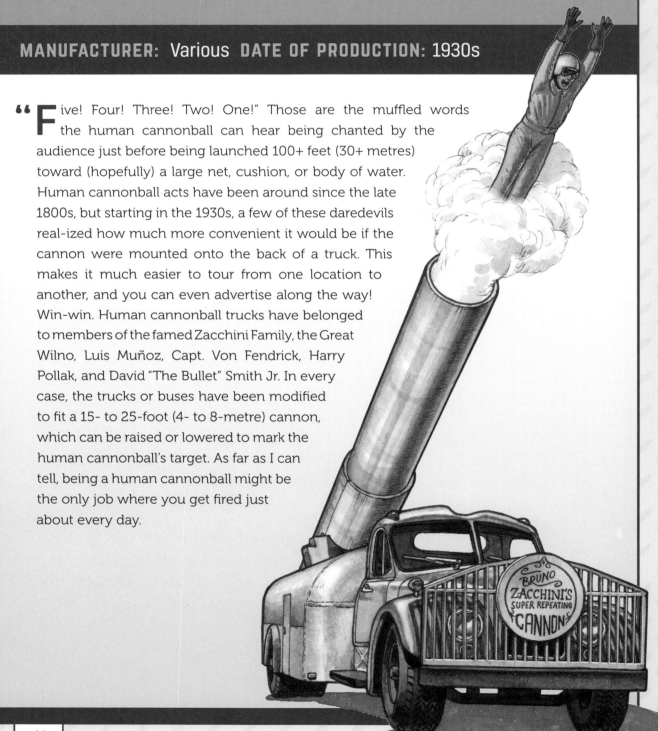

"Five! Four! Three! Two! One!" Those are the muffled words the human cannonball can hear being chanted by the audience just before being launched 100+ feet (30+ metres) toward (hopefully) a large net, cushion, or body of water. Human cannonball acts have been around since the late 1800s, but starting in the 1930s, a few of these daredevils real-ized how much more convenient it would be if the cannon were mounted onto the back of a truck. This makes it much easier to tour from one location to another, and you can even advertise along the way! Win-win. Human cannonball trucks have belonged to members of the famed Zacchini Family, the Great Wilno, Luis Muñoz, Capt. Von Fendrick, Harry Pollak, and David "The Bullet" Smith Jr. In every case, the trucks or buses have been modified to fit a 15- to 25-foot (4- to 8-metre) cannon, which can be raised or lowered to mark the human cannonball's target. As far as I can tell, being a human cannonball might be the only job where you get fired just about every day.

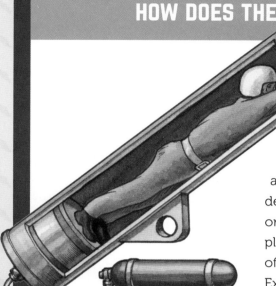

I knew you'd ask. It's a trade secret, and no human cannonball is going to tell you! But I can at least say that it's not really a "cannon," since a propellant is not used to project the person. "Catapult" would be a better word. Various performers have used various designs, but almost all have used some form of spring or compressed air to quickly push an inner chamber or platform forward. When the chamber reaches the end of the tube, it stops . . . and the human keeps going! Exploding gunpowder is often added just for effect.

A FEW THINGS YOU SHOULD KNOW BEFORE CANNONBALLING . . .

$$R = \frac{v_0{}^2 \sin 2\theta}{g}$$

1. Apparently it doesn't feel so great to be launched from a cannon. Shawn Marren, "The Sorcerer of the Stratosphere," explains that he locks every muscle he can possibly lock while traveling from 0 to 60 miles (97 kilometres) per hour in just a quarter of a second!

2. The current distance record of any human cannonball is 193 feet, 8.8 inches (59 metres, 22 centimetres), claimed by David "The Bullet" Smith Jr.

3. Of all the human cannonballs out there (it's speculated to be a little more than 100 people throughout history), more than 30 have died from mishaps. In other words, there are safer jobs out there.

4. The kinematic equation for calculating where to place your landing cushion is in the equation above, where "R" is the horizontal distance from the muzzle of the cannon, "v0" is the initial velocity, "g" is the acceleration due to gravity, and "θ" is the launch angle . . . just in case you needed to know. Again, I don't recommend you launch yourself from a cannon.*

*This equation doesn't take into account wind resistance or common sense.

HYPERLOOP

MANUFACTURER: Virgin Hyperloop One and others **DATE OF PRODUCTION:** 2015–present

Is the Hyperloop our future? Or will it go down the tubes? There's certainly a ton of research going into this new form of transportation. But would you travel in a pod through a near-vacuum tube from one city to another at up to 670 miles (1,078 kilometres) per hour? We're talking San Francisco to Los Angeles in under an hour—a trip that normally takes six hours by car (in no traffic). Sounds good to me! In 2017, Hyperloop One, the current leader of the Hyperloop race, successfully sent a 28-foot (8.5-metre) pod through its 1,640-foot (500-metre) test *tube* in the Nevada desert. *Boom!* There are still many hurdles to overcome before you and I are riding in a Hyperloop. For example: negotiating with public agencies in each city, and raising insane amounts of money to build stations as well as some seriously looooong tubes. I suppose if all else fails, we'll at least get an awesome amusement ride in the Nevada desert.

I SMELL A BILLIONAIRE (OR TWO)

Although the initial concept dates back to 1904, when physicist Robert Goddard came up with the idea for a "vactrain," Elon Musk (along with SpaceX and Tesla) first proposed the Hyperloop in 2012. More recently, Richard Branson and the Virgin Group have jumped on board.

BELIEVE THE HYPE(RLOOP)!

Unlike the pneumatic tubes used by your bank (wait, does your bank still use pneumatic tubes?), the Hyperloop is not propelled by air pressure. Instead, it runs using a linear electromagnetic motor. The near vacuum inside the tube creates very little air resistance, which allows for high speeds using the smallest amount of electricity. The pod also magnetically levitates above the track to further reduce friction. In other words, it's magic.

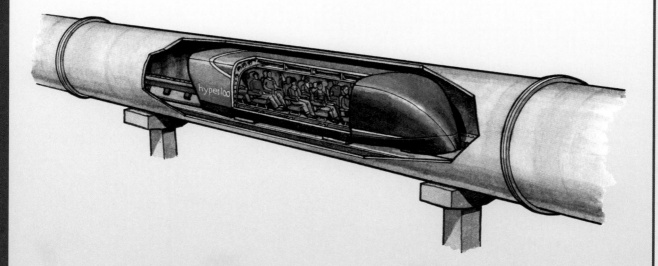

In 2015, students and non-student teams began participating in a SpaceX design competition to build the best Hyperloop pod. The winner of the competion gets, uh, to brag that they built the best pod.

HZ-1 AEROCYCLE

MANUFACTURER: de Lackner Helicopters **DATE OF PRODUCTION:** 1954–1956

US ARM

Who wants a personal helicopter? Me! Though I might pass on *this* one, considering the pilot is required to stand directly above two high-speed rotor blades. Yikes! Manufactured by de Lackner Helicopters, this flying machine made a brief appearance when the U.S. Army ordered 12 units back in the 1950s. One brave (or foolish) man named Captain Selmer Sundby volunteered to test the Aerocycle at Fort Eustis in Virginia. Sundby held on to the motorcycle-like handlebars, taking numerous flights (one lasting 43 minutes). Twice, however, he had accidents—both times, the counter-rotating blades collided into each other and shattered. Sundby was unharmed, but the HZ-1 project was forever abandoned. Perhaps for the best.

DON'T THINK SO

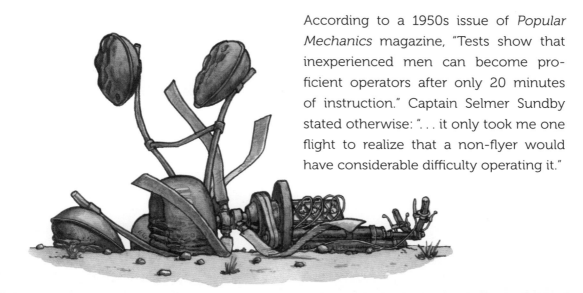

According to a 1950s issue of *Popular Mechanics* magazine, "Tests show that inexperienced men can become proficient operators after only 20 minutes of instruction." Captain Selmer Sundby stated otherwise: ". . . it only took me one flight to realize that a non-flyer would have considerable difficulty operating it."

AND YET!

During its test phase, the HZ-1 Aerocycle flew over 160 flights with more than 15 hours of flying time. Supposedly, the craft could travel up to 15 miles (24 kilometres), at speeds of more than 70 miles (113 kilometres) per hour, at an altitude of 5,000 feet (1,500 metres).

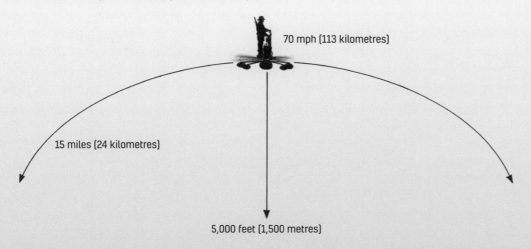

70 mph (113 kilometres)

15 miles (24 kilometres)

5,000 feet (1,500 metres)

JAIL WAGON

MANUFACTURER: Various **DATE OF PRODUCTION:** Various

Did you know there was a time before cars and trucks? Of course you did. Automobiles, as we know them, have only been around since the 1800s. On the other hand (or hoof), horse-drawn vehicles date back 5,000 years! That's right—chariots, fire engines, stagecoaches, hearses, and even police wagons were all once pulled by horses.

The jail wagon was used to transport prisoners short distances—from country jail to state penitentiary, or from the train station to the penitentiary. And what better way to keep citizens from the wrong side of the law than to see a horse-drawn wagon pass by with an angry prisoner yelling through the bars? As it was said, there's always room for one more . . .

HORSEPOWER! HORSEPOWER?

Turns out one horsepower doesn't really equal the power of one horse. The term refers to the amount of power a horse could sustain over a period of time. To be specific, one horsepower is equal to 550 foot-pounds per second, or 745.7 watts. Based on that *simple* math, a horse is actually capable of approximately 14.9 horsepower. Wait, what?

AND NOW FOR A SHORT DERIVATIVE POEM . . .

A horse is a horse, of course, of course,

before we had engines, the horse was the source,

of power to transport a criminal force,

which probably furthered the prisoners' remorse.

TUMBLEWEED WAGON

Yep, that's another name for this vehicle. Apparently, like real tumbleweed, these wagons would often wander randomly through the open prairie, looking for bad people.

JET PACK

MANUFACTURER: Bell, JetPack Aviation, Martin Aircraft Co., and others **DATE OF PRODUCTION:** 1959–present

We've been waiting and waiting. Where's my jet pack? Comic books and science fiction have teased us for years. In the early 1960s, things *started* to get real when the Bell "Rocket Belt" made numerous demonstrations. Unfortunately, it turns out the human body is rather difficult to control in jet pack flight. Additionally, the weight of the person plus the weight of the pack—along with 5 gallons (19 litres) of hydrogen peroxide fuel—only allowed for short flights (10 to 25 seconds). Whatever. I still want my jet pack! More than half a century later, in 2015, pilot David Mayman and engineer Nelson Tyler presented the JB-9 jet pack with twin turbine engines and a carbon fiber corset, which Mayman flew for several minutes in front of the Statue of Liberty. Sweet! Next up, the JB-10, which is reported to fly at 68 miles (109 kilometres) per hour for up to 10 minutes (depending on your weight). Currently, the JB-11 is in production, featuring six smaller engines and built-in auto-stabilization. I don't know about you, but I'm starting to feel jet-pack-jazzed once again!

WANTED
Working (practical)
Jet Pack!

REWARD
$2,000,000

In 2017, Boeing offered a $2 million prize for a "working, easy-to-use, personal flying device." (They were calling for a jet pack.) "It must be safe, quiet, and carry a person at least 20 miles (32 kilometres) without refueling." So far, nobody has claimed the reward.

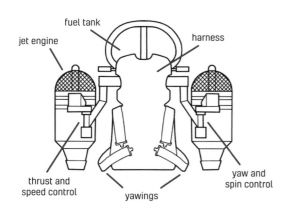

fuel tank

jet engine

harness

thrust and
speed control

yawings

yaw and
spin control

HOW TO JOCKEY A JET PACK

The JB-10 jet pack is controlled using handheld levers. The right lever is twisted for throttle (thrust and speed), and the left is twisted for direction (it changes the position of the yawings on the bottom of the jets). This, in combination with the pilot shifting her/his weight, allows for maneuvering.

A FEW OTHER PERSONAL FLYING DEVICES

Bell "Rocket Belt": The original! As seen in the James Bond film *Thunderball*, and in the 1984 Los Angeles Summer Olympics opening ceremony. Oh, yeah, and Michael Jackson's Dangerous tour. P.S. No, that wasn't MJ flying the rocket belt. It was stuntman Kinnie Gibson.

Martin Jet Pack: Using gasoline and two fans, this isn't exactly a "jet pack." But it is said it travels as high as 2,500 feet (762 metres) for around 30 minutes. Needless to say, it's not one of the most portable personal flying devices out there.

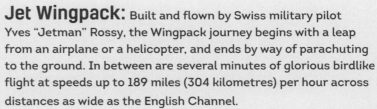

Jet Wingpack: Built and flown by Swiss military pilot Yves "Jetman" Rossy, the Wingpack journey begins with a leap from an airplane or a helicopter, and ends by way of parachuting to the ground. In between are several minutes of glorious birdlike flight at speeds up to 189 miles (304 kilometres) per hour across distances as wide as the English Channel.

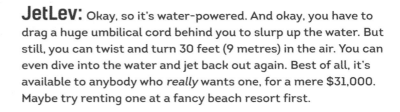

JetLev: Okay, so it's water-powered. And okay, you have to drag a huge umbilical cord behind you to slurp up the water. But still, you can twist and turn 30 feet (9 metres) in the air. You can even dive into the water and jet back out again. Best of all, it's available to anybody who *really* wants one, for a mere $31,000. Maybe try renting one at a fancy beach resort first.

JET TRAIN

MANUFACTURER: New York City Railroad Corporation **DATE OF PRODUCTION:** 1966

Jet engines on a train? Why not! The M-497, created by the New York City Railroad Corporation, had exactly that— two J47-19 Air Force jet engines mounted on top of a Budd commuter car. It was nicknamed the "Black Beetle" by the press, and off it went on a series of test drives between Butler, Indiana, and Stryker, Ohio, reaching a maximum speed of 183.681 miles (295.606 kilometres) per hour. Unfortunately, the idea of the jet train never caught on. The engines were ultimately removed, and the train was returned to its former life as a diesel locomotive. From this experiment, however, we learned that many of the tracks of 1966 could handle high-speed rail. And yet . . . we *still* don't have high-speed rail in America! Hello?

COLD WAR COMBO

Yup, the Soviet Union also felt the need to make one. The ER22 was built in 1970 and reached a speed of 154 miles (248 kilometres) per hour. However, it was too expensive (and too loud) to operate. To this day, the Soviet rocket train sits on an abandoned track, collecting rust.

MEANWHILE

While the Soviet Union and America were duking it out over jet trains, Japan was working on its Shinkansen bullet train, and France on its TGV, both of which are much faster and are still in use today.

KRUPP BAGGER 288

MANUFACTURER: Krupp DATE OF PRODUCTION: 1978

If you ever find yourself in the coal mines of western Germany and this 705-foot-long, 311-foot-tall, 27-million-pound (215-metre-long, 95-metre-tall, 12-million-kilogram) excavator comes your way, you might consider taking a big step aside. The Bagger 288 (one of several baggers built by the Krupp company), with its 18-bucket circular digger, can scoop out a 30-foot- (9-metre-) deep hole the width and length of a football field in just one day! It also has a built-in conveyor-belt system to haul away the 240,000 tons (218,000 metric tons) of coal it excavates. And when the coal's all gone (which tends to happen), the bagger can crawl to a new site. Like a mobile city with a giant buzz saw on one end, this monster travels at a maximum speed of about a ½ mile (1 kilometre) per hour—that means it can take nearly a week just to move a few miles (kilometres). Wake me up when we get there!

Power Loop

The coal that the 288 digs up is loaded onto trains and hauled to nearby power stations. The bagger then draws its power from these very same stations. How confusing is that?

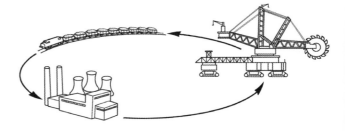

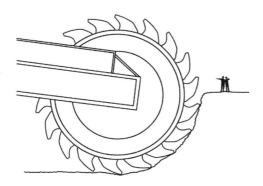

The 18-bucket digger and two tiny dudes

FOUR FUN FACTS (AND ONE NOT-SO-FUN FACT)

1. The word "bagger" is German for "excavator."

2. Although the 288 is heavier than the Eiffel Tower and taller than the Statue of Liberty, only three or four people operate this goliath machine at any given time.

3. The bucket wheel alone is 71 feet (22 metres) tall, which is about the height of a seven-story building.

4. Only a few vehicles are larger than the Krupp Bagger 288, one being the Krupp Bagger 293 (which, in my opinion, isn't as cool-looking as the 288). And then there's the Overburden Conveyor Bridge F60—a large movable bridge and conveyor system also used for mining—and NASA's Crawler Transporters, which haul rockets out to the launch pad at Cape Canaveral.

5. Each ton (0.9 metric ton) of coal dug up by the bagger and burned at a power station releases more than 2 tons (1.8 metric tons) of carbon dioxide into the atmosphere. Perhaps you've heard of a little thing called climate change?

LIBERTY ONE STEAM-POWERED ROCKET

MANUFACTURER: Mad Mike Hughes **DATE OF PRODUCTION:** 2016–2018

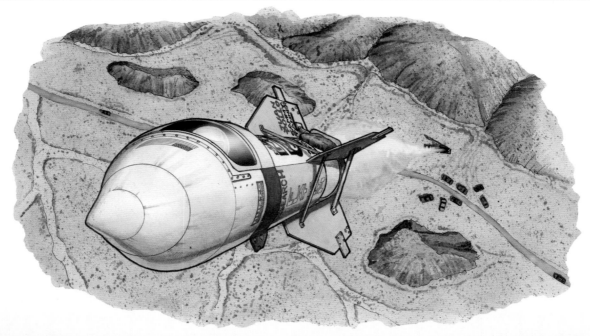

Want to launch yourself in a home-made steam-powered rocket? According to Liberty One's builder and pilot, Mad Mike Hughes, "This thing wants to kill you ten different ways." On March, 24, 2018, with a loud *WHOOOOSH*, the super-heated water-propelled Liberty One took off for the second time with 7,100 pounds (3,200 kilograms) of thrust, reaching an altitude of 1,875 feet (572 metres) above the Mojave Desert in a matter of seconds. And then it was already time for the descent.

The first parachute was immediately deployed (perhaps too soon); however, Liberty One was falling at 350 miles (563 kilometres) per hour. A second parachute was released moments before a rather hard landing. A third launch, in February 2020, ended in tragedy. The world will miss Mad Mike—for his ingenuity, his daring, and his sense of humor.

NOT ROCKET SCIENCE

Although Mike Hughes had no formal education in rocketry (in fact, he was a limousine driver by day), he managed to build several steam-powered rockets using aluminum, hand grinders, and cutting wheels.

WAIT, IS THE EARTH FLAT?

Raising money to build a rocket can be challenging . . . which is why Mike decided to join up with a larger force such as, um, the Flat Earth Society—a group determined to prove millions of scientists wrong. What better way to confirm that the Earth is flat than to send someone up in a rocket to see it with their own eyes? Oh, wait—we already did that, and it turns out the Earth is a sphere.

IN MEMORIAM: A PHONE CALL WITH MAD MIKE HUGHES.*

ME: What do you think of Evel Knievel?
MAD MIKE: He's not qualified to tie my shoelaces.

ME: Do you really think the Earth is flat?
MAD MIKE: I'm not saying I believe it, just research it. Make your own decision. Question everything.

ME: Did you study rocketry?
MAD MIKE: I don't believe in science, I believe in formulas.

ME: What formulas did you use?
MAD MIKE: We were still doing the math on this thing the day I launched. I didn't give anyone a countdown, because that's nobody's business.

ME: Why didn't you use rocket fuel?
MAD MIKE: Water is cheaper.

*This is verbatim.

LOCKHEED XFV

MANUFACTURER: Lockheed **DATE OF PRODUCTION:** 1951–1954

Vertical takeoff: It's not just for rockets! Did you know there's a whole category of aircraft known as VTOL? Vertical Take-Off and Landing aircraft. Makes sense to me—an aircraft that can take off from a ship deck or other tight space without a runway. How convenient! Nazi Germany had the idea for a tail-sitting aircraft called the Triebflügel back in the 1940s. Although it was never fully built, the plans, which were discovered by Allied forces, "inspired" the U.S. Navy to work on a few similar concepts, including the Lockheed XFV. The XFV was powered by a turboprop engine connected to two sets of contra-rotating propellers. A single pilot sat facing the sky and revved the engines until liftoff. After 32 test flights, it was decided that the aircraft was *way* too difficult to control (especially landing), and the engine was prone to troubles. Oh, well. A stepping-stone in the process—a process that has given us other successful VTOL aircraft, including the Harrier Jet and the V-22 Osprey.

FLIGHT OF THE XFV (IDEALLY)

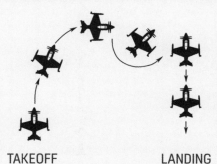

TAKEOFF   LANDING

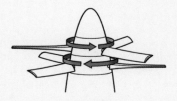

Contra-rotation

DID YOU KNOW?

1. The chief test pilot for the XFV was Herman "Fish" Salmon. That's why the XFV is also known as the salmon.

2. Lockheed employees also joked and called it the pogo stick.

3. Contra-rotating propellers may be more efficient than normal propellers, but their complexity and weight make the improvement in efficiency negligible.

SNECMA C.450 COLÉOPTÈRE

Another early attempt at a VTOL aircraft: the "beetle," powered by a single turbojet, first flew in 1958. It made eight successful flights before it lost control and crashed.

NOT SO SUCCESSFUL

BELL BOEING V-22 OSPREY

Essentially a combination of a helicopter and an airplane, this craft's rotors swivel from vertical to horizontal during flight!

SUCCESSFUL

MONOWHEEL

MANUFACTURER: Various **DATE OF PRODUCTION:** c. 1869–present

The wheel was invented over 5,000 years ago. Ever since then, we humans have thought of countless ways to use this very basic invention, in particular with vehicles. At some point (more recently), someone thought, why not sit inside the wheel and drive *that*? I mean, really, what more do you need? Turns out a lot. For example: visibility, stability, steering, and the ability to quickly start and stop without "gerbiling." Nonetheless, between the 1860s and the 1930s, the monowheel (also referred to as a monocycle) was frequently suggested as a serious new form of transportation. Numerous inventors came up with their own versions of the monowheel—some human-powered, some electric, some with gas motors—all working off the same basic principle: The driver sits within a smaller inner ring, which presses against the main outer wheel, allowing the vehicle to roll forward while the driver remains level. Unfortunately (or fortunately?), the monowheel never really caught on. However, to this day, people still build and attempt to drive these roly-polies . . . though usually just for entertainment. They certainly entertain *me*.

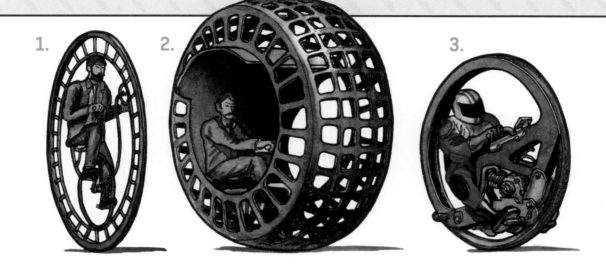

1. Rousseau of Marseilles's monowheel (1869): Pedal power!

2. Dr. J. H. Purves's Dynasphere (1932): Could reach 30 miles (48 kilometres) per hour, but was nearly impossible to steer or brake.

3. The UK Monowheel Team's WarHorse (2015): The current fastest monowheel at 61 miles (98 kilometres) per hour.

GERBILING

Couldn't they have come up with a better word? For a monowheeler, it's when the driver accelerates or brakes too quickly, and as a result (from inertia) ends up spinning inside the wheel. The term itself refers to what might happen to a gerbil running too quickly inside an exercise wheel.

A MONO-VERSED POEM

My monowheel is quite ideal.
I'd offer you a ride . . .
but it cannot turn, it has no brakes,
and only *I* can fit inside!

MOON BUGGY

MANUFACTURER: Boeing / General Motors **DATE OF PRODUCTION:** 1971–1972

Dude! It's the farthest-from-Earth human-operated vehicle. The moon buggy! Technically, it's called the Lunar Roving Vehicle (LRV) . . . but *moon buggy* is so much more fun to say, don't you think? Three LRVs have been brought to the moon aboard Apollo missions 15, 16, and 17. The LRVs were unpacked on the surface of the moon, and then driven around by one or two astronauts, allowing them to explore and collect lunar samples. To this day, the buggies remain parked on the surface of the moon, waiting for YOU to take them for a spin.

MOON BUGGY FACTS

- In total, five buggies have been driven on the moon—three by the United States, and two by the Soviet Union. China also landed a buggy on the moon in 2013, but it was unmanned.

- The moon buggy hit a top speed of 11.2 miles (18 kilometres) per hour by astronaut Eugene Cernan.

- The astronaut controls the buggy using a T-shaped joystick-like device.

- The total distance traveled by all three LRVs was about 56 miles (90 kilometres) over the course of 11 hours of combined driving time.

HOW TO GET A MOON BUGGY TO THE MOON IN FIVE NOT-SO-EASY STEPS

1. Blast off from Earth using a Saturn V rocket (the largest and most powerful rocket ever built).

2. After all three fuel stages have been used, release the command module, turn around and grab the lunar module, turn back around, and then soar toward the moon at 240,000 miles (386,000 kilometres) per hour for 3 days.

3. Once the moon's orbit has been reached, deploy the lunar module and carefully descend to the surface.

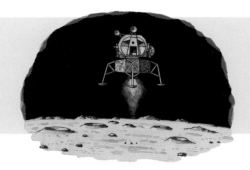

4. After landing, climb out and unfold the LRV (moon buggy) from the side of the lunar module.

5. Enjoy the ride, you lucky astronaut! (Good luck getting back to Earth.)

ONEWHEEL ELECTRIC RIDEABLE

MANUFACTURER: Future Motion Inc.   **DATE OF PRODUCTION:** 2013–present

Seems like we're suddenly motorizing every type of bicycle, scooter, and pair of roller skates out there. Are we just too lazy to use our own muscles? Or maybe these inventions are simply that *awesome* and *fun*! The "rideable movement," as I'm now officially calling it, is likely the result of batteries and electric motors becoming smaller, cheaper, and more powerful. But with so many options of rideables, which one will still be around in 20 years? The Onewheel (not to be confused with the monowheel on page 62) certainly seems like a solid contender. With its extra-large (and only) wheel, it has the ability to roll over bumpy roads, wet ground, and even grass and dirt. Of course, there's likely a bit of a learning curve with that whole balance thing for many people. But I'm guessing skateboarders, snowboarders, and surfers will quickly catch on and find the appeal. Not to mention the bonus of receiving perplexed looks from passers-by.

"RIDEABLES" Yep, that's the word of choice these days. Some people also refer to them as "personal transport gadgets." But that's three words, and "rideables" is only one.

A FEW OTHER RIDEABLES INCLUDE . . .

Electric Skateboards

Many, many brands out there. Boosted, Swagtron, LOU, and Blink, to name a few.

Electric Scooters

Skinny wheels, fat wheels, seats, fold-up, you name it, from companies such as Razor, Gotrax, Glion Dolly, and Qiewa.

Rideable Carry-On Luggage

I kid you not. Drive the Modobag motorized suitcase right to your gate. It's TSA compliant and even fits in the overhead bin!

Electric Roller Skates

Introducing Action RocketSkates, yet another fine product brought to you by Shark Tank.

Electric Unicycle

Step aside, *old* Segway, and meet the Segway One S1 unicycle.

OSTRICH CARRIAGE

MANUFACTURER: Humans **DATE OF PRODUCTION:** Unknown

Horses, mules, oxen, and many other animals (including humans) have all been used to pull carts since the invention of the wheel (see page 62). But how about these feathered non-flyers? Yep, ostriches have done their share of bridled labor too, most notably in the late 1800s and early 1900s, in the form of "ostrich races" at such locations as the Santa Ana Racetrack in California and the Monroe County Fairgrounds in Rochester, New York. The oversized birds were typically harnessed with blindfolds on, and attached to carriages known as sulkies. After the jockey took his seat in the sulky, the temperamental birds would be lined up at the starting gate, and the blindfolds would quickly be removed. *And they're off!* Did I mention that the jockeys had no brakes or any way of steering?

BIRDBRAINS

In 1896, an Anaheim, California, barber named Billy Frantz and a postman named Frank Eastman purchased two ostriches (which they named Napoleon and Josephine). The men trained the birds to pull a sulky, and sent them to various races, competing against bicycles, horses, and who knows what else. The ostriches mostly won! That is, until Napoleon and Josephine figured out that they could stop a race at any time by simply sitting down.

TRUE OR FALSE?

1. Ostriches' high-speed running is aided by having only two toes on each foot. The larger inner toe acts similarly to a hoof.

2. Ostriches are the fastest runners of any bird (or two-legged animal, for that matter) and can move over 43 miles (69 kilometres) per hour!

3. Ostriches often run when feeling threatened. They can also use their legs to kick a predator or enemy (including a human).

4. When *really* scared, ostriches will run and lay eggs at the same time. These eggs are more than triple their normal size.

5. I, Michael Hearst, the author of this book, have also written a book about strange animals called *Unusual Creatures*.

Answers: 1. True. [Most birds have four.] 2. Yup. True. 3. True. Napoleon the ostrich kicked Billy Frantz in the head one time during a feeding and nearly killed him. 4. False. But I wouldn't be surprised if an ostrich or two has laid an egg while running scared. 5. True. This is a cheap plug for you to check out that book, too.

RIPSAW

MANUFACTURER: Howe and Howe Technologies   **DATE OF PRODUCTION:** 2009-present

Twin brothers Mike and Geoff Howe like to build high-tech armored vehicles. Among their arsenal is the Ripsaw, an extreme vehicle that cranks out up to 1,500 horsepower (1,119 kilowatts) and is able to reach 62 miles (100 kilometres) per hour in 3.2 seconds. Holy heck, that's a lot of horses! This nearly unstoppable supertank comes in a variety of styles, from the unmanned UGV, MS1, MS2, and MS3 models, to the multiseated EV1, EV2, and EV3 luxury tanks (because sometimes you need a luxury tank!). Do YOU have a *crushing* desire to drive over just about everything and anything in your way? Buckle up: A Ripsaw can be yours for $295,000.

TWO MUCH TROUBLE?

It's only fitting that twin brothers who make extreme vehicles would also play in a band called Two Much Trouble. At least, they did when they were younger. And wouldn't you know it, they built their own extreme mobile stage . . . out of a school bus!

AN UNCONVENTIONAL BACKLOT TOUR

Hey, fans of *Mad Max: Fury Road* and *G.I. Joe: Retaliation*, the Ripsaw was featured in both films! In the latter, the Rock (Dwayne Douglas Johnson) was supposed to drive the Ripsaw, but then Mike Howe stepped in as the stunt driver. Throughout production, Mike was apparently referred to as the Boulder.

ROADS? WHERE WE'RE GOING, WE DON'T NEED ROADS.

In addition to the Ripsaw, Howe and Howe Technologies has manufactured such unconventional vehicles as the THERMITE—an unmanned robotic firefighting tank for up-close battles with scorching fires; the BADGER—the world's smallest one-man armored tank (capable of plowing through cinderblock walls); and the RIPCHAIR—an extreme off-roading vehicle designed to fit a wheelchair-bound adventurist.

SCUBADOO

MANUFACTURER: Scubadoo **DATE OF PRODUCTION:** 2003

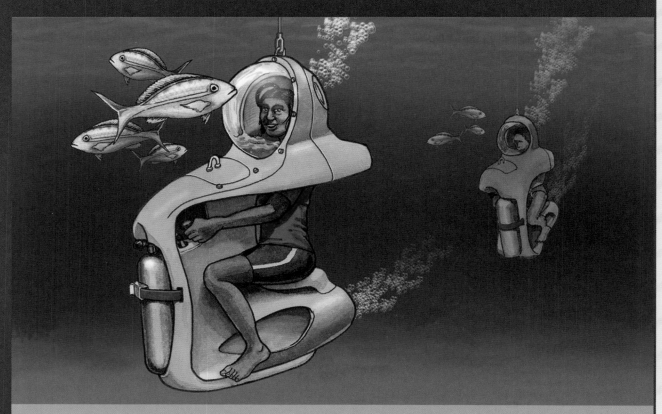

You know you want one. An underwater battery-powered scooter! Cruise in comfort alongside sea turtles and tropical fish while breathing just like you do on land. A scuba tank under the handlebars sends air into the head dome, allowing you to breathe without help from a mask or other breathing apparatus. The dome is also wired so you can talk to other riders or a companion back on the boat. Take your time—less kicking and paddling means less oxygen consumption, allowing you to stay submerged for about an hour. Pretty cool! Although the Scubadoo website says "No swimming experience required," I might suggest otherwise . . . just to be safe.

NO NEED FOR SPEED

The Scubadoo breathing observation bubble (BOB) has a top speed of about 3 miles (5 kilometres) per hour. All good—just take in the view. It is also set to a fixed depth of 13 feet (4 metres). And yes, for safety purposes, it's typically tethered to a buoy.

CLAUSTROPHOBIC?

If so, this might not be for you. There have been reports that using the BOB is similar to sticking your head inside an empty fish bowl. I can't imagine why.

HEAD DOME? HEAD BUBBLE?

Well, what would you call it? While riding the Scubadoo, your head and shoulders are in a water-free dome-bubble. The scuba tank is constantly replenishing the air inside the dome-bubble.

SOLAR-POWERED RACE CAR

MANUFACTURER: Various **DATE OF PRODUCTION:** c. 1985 (first solar-car race)

Yup, it's a thing. A race car powered by the sun! At the time of writing this book, the high-speed record was 56.75 miles (91 kilometres) per hour, achieved by Kenjiro Shinozuka of Japan, in a three-wheeled car called Sky Ace TIGA. Not bad for a SUNday drive! Although the first solar car dates back to 1955, solar-car racing started in 1985 in Switzerland, and soon spread to other parts of Europe, Asia, Australia, and the United States. In almost all cases, the cars have a single battery that is charged when sunlight hits the solar panels. This battery allows the vehicle to maintain power even when a massive cloud gets in the way. The key to speed with these cars is making them extremely light and aerodynamic, while having a solar array that's as large as possible. The more solar panels, the more sunlight that's harnessed, the more energy! Even then, the cars run on about the same amount of power as a toaster. I imagine the drivers inside these suncatchers also *feel* like they're inside a toaster!

WATCH OUT FOR KANGAROOS, PLEASE!

The biggest solar-car challenge in the world is conveniently called the World Solar Challenge. This 1,864-mile (3,000-kilometre) race travels the entire length of Australia—from Darwin to Adelaide—a journey that takes four to six days.

FAMILY FUN IN THE SUN

Although solar race cars are too dangerous for general consumers, solar-powered family cars (which can fit four people and still have room for groceries) are currently being engineered at places such as Eindhoven University of Technology in the Netherlands. Go, Solar Team Eindhoven, go!

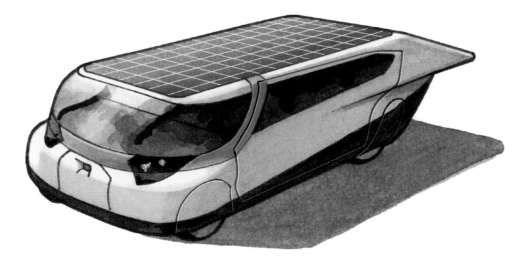

 **P.S.** Did you know that "race car" spelled backward is "race car"?

STOOPIDTALLER™

MANUFACTURER: Richie Trimble **DATE OF PRODUCTION:** 2013

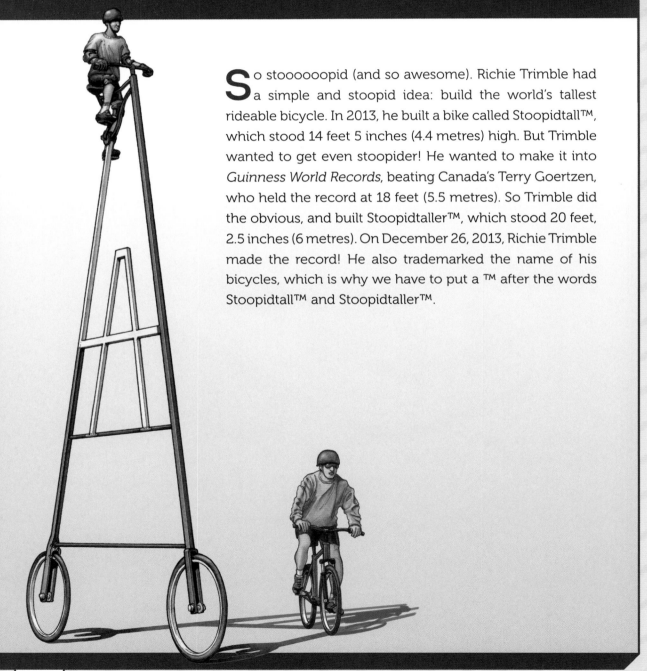

So stooooooopid (and so awesome). Richie Trimble had a simple and stoopid idea: build the world's tallest rideable bicycle. In 2013, he built a bike called Stoopidtall™, which stood 14 feet 5 inches (4.4 metres) high. But Trimble wanted to get even stoopider! He wanted to make it into *Guinness World Records*, beating Canada's Terry Goertzen, who held the record at 18 feet (5.5 metres). So Trimble did the obvious, and built Stoopidtaller™, which stood 20 feet, 2.5 inches (6 metres). On December 26, 2013, Richie Trimble made the record! He also trademarked the name of his bicycles, which is why we have to put a ™ after the words Stoopidtall™ and Stoopidtaller™.

DANDY FACT

The award for earliest (verified) bicycle goes to Karl von Drais for his Laufmaschine (running machine), which was invented in 1817. The following year, he patented the two-wheeled, human-propelled machine, which became commonly known as a *draisine* or dandy horse.

STOOPID DREAMS DON'T ALWAYS COME TRUE

In 2008, Michael Mooney rode a 43-foot (13-metre) bicycle in Asheville, North Carolina. Unfortunately, he was unable to ride the full 100 metres (328 feet) required by *Guinness World Records*.

StoopidTall™
14 ft, 5 in (4.39 m)

Goertzen Bike
18 ft (5.49 m)

StoopidTaller™
20 ft, 2.5 in (6.15 m)

Mooney Bike
43 ft (13 m)

P.S. I love the word "stoopid." Of course, the real word is "stupid." But when you swap the "u" for two "o"s, it becomes even stoopider! According to urbandictionary.com, it's "when something is just so dumb and lacking any common sense that 'stupid' doesn't seem to cut it."

STROLLON STROLLER

MANUFACTURER: Yanko Design **DATE OF PRODUCTION:** 2013

A space-age stroller for the luckiest kid in the world! French designer Amir Labidi knows how much children love vehicles. So why not make a stroller with a windshield, side windows, a removable door, and a sporty exterior? Done! Welcome to the future, wee human.

"HAPPY KIDS MAKE HAPPY PARENTS"

So it says on the Strollon website. (And yes, I can attest that it certainly helps.) Most strollers are designed with the parents in mind. This one, however, was clearly built for the kid's enjoyment. Can I still at least have a coffee holder, pretty please?

FALSE, FALSE, OR FALSE?

1. The stroller comes equipped with a pair of detachable class-4 laser guns to combat automobiles that refuse to give pedestrians the right-of-way.

2. After reports of diaper aisles being knocked down due to shock waves from the stroller's sonic booms (see page 19), safety guidelines were placed on the Strollon to keep the speed just below 767.269 miles (1,234.799 kilometres) per hour.

3. Elon Musk and Richard Branson have joined forces, commissioning Yanko Design to manufacture a self-sustainable Strollon that will be capable of easily navigating the rocky surface of Mars.

Answers: 1. False. 2. False. 3. False.

CHECK IT OUT!

Just as there's a first verified bicycle (see page 77), there's also a first verified baby carriage. It was built in 1773 by English architect and furniture designer William Kent for the third Duke of Devonshire's children. The carriage was designed to be pulled by a dog, a goat, or a miniature horse!

SWALLOWABLE WIRELESS CAMERA

MANUFACTURER: Given Imaging (now Medtronic)   **DATE OF PRODUCTION:** 1997–present

Yep, it's a vehicle. A very *small* vehicle. Personally, I hate taking pills. Especially large pills. But I guess sometimes there's no way around it. And now there's a pill you can swallow that's actually a mini wireless camera! Should your doctor need to look at your intestines, well, now you can gulp down this little bugger, which will take photographs of your innards and transmit them (up to six per second) to a portable recording device worn on your belt. The pillcam will drift through your digestive track, filming until the battery runs out, usually about eight hours, which is enough to make one epic movie about your entrails. The doctor can then review the footage to look for bleeding, polyps, tumors, and just about any other nasty thing that might cause abdominal distress.

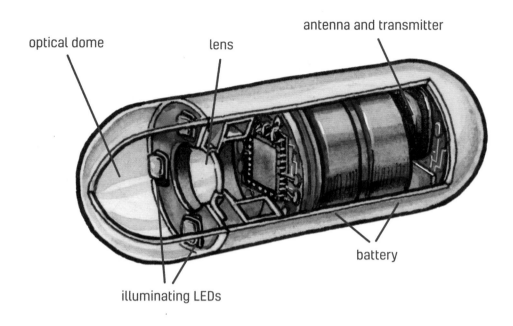

optical dome

lens

antenna and transmitter

illuminating LEDs

battery

HOW DOES THE PILLCAM GET OUT OF THE BODY?

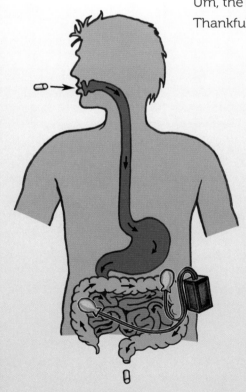

Um, the same way all undigested food gets out of your body. Thankfully, the camera is not reusable.

FANTASTIC VOYAGE?

Or at least a fantastic advance in medical science. Apparently this camera capsule is much more gentle on the intestines than the classic endoscope (a small camera attached to a wire that is hand-fed down the intestine).

THE ONE PERCENT

Okay, there *have* been a few reports of pillcams getting stuck in people's bodies for as long as three months, resulting in emergency camera removal surgery . . . a procedure that I hereby abbreviate to ECRS.

THE TURTLE

MANUFACTURER: David Bushnell   **DATE OF PRODUCTION:** 1775

I know what you're thinking: *It doesn't look like a turtle!* Perhaps more like a barnacle? More importantly, this is the first documented submersible to be used in battle. It's a one-person-operated wooden ball that's capable of attaching explosives to the bottoms of unsuspecting ships. At least, that's what it *tried* to do during the American War of Independence. On September 6, 1776, using foot pedals and hand cranks, Sgt. Ezra Lee piloted the Turtle through the rough waters of New York harbor to the British Navel ship *Eagle*, which was moored just off Governors Island. Lee made every effort to drill the explosives to the underside of the ship, but failed (likely because the hull was made of metal), and was forced to retreat due to diminishing air. Nonetheless, the Turtle goes down in history as an essential part of the evolution of modern submarines and submersible combat.

EFFORT OF GENIUS!

David Bushnell, an American inventor from Connecticut, conceived of the Turtle. He proposed his invention to the Connecticut governor, Jonathan Trumbull. Trumbull, in turn, recommended it to George Washington, who approved funding for the project. Despite the Turtle's missed moment, Washington referred to the invention as "an effort of genius." I must agree.

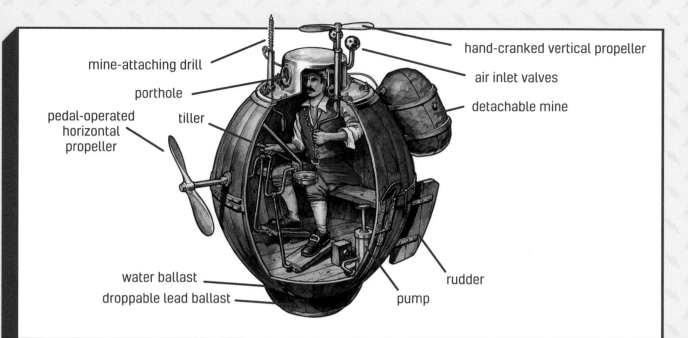

mine-attaching drill

porthole

pedal-operated
horizontal
propeller

tiller

hand-cranked vertical propeller

air inlet valves

detachable mine

water ballast

droppable lead ballast

pump

rudder

TOTALLY RIDICULOUS AND AWESOME OPERATING PROCEDURES FOR THE TURTLE

▪ The operator pumped water in and out of the ballast tank in order to navigate the vessel to the proper depth.

▪ The vessel was driven vertically and horizontally by hand-cranked and foot-pedaled propellers, reaching a speed of approximately 3 miles (5 kilometres) per hour.

▪ The Turtle was steered by a hand-held tiller connected to a rudder.

▪ Once at the base of a ship, a keg of wooden gunpowder would be attached by a hand-cranked drill, and then the explosives would be lit using a really long fuse.

▪ All of this needed to be done before the Turtle ran out of air (approximately 30 minutes).

TWO TIDBITS FROM 200+ YEARS LATER . . .

1. In 2007, artist Duke Riley launched a replica of the Turtle into the waters of Red Hook, Brooklyn. As he neared the British cruise ship *Queen Mary 2*, he was arrested by police and issued a citation for violating the *QM2*'s security zone. The sub, which carried no threatening devices, was impounded.

2. In 2019, among the equipment at J. J. Byrne Playground in Brooklyn is a large plastic map of New York Harbor, which allows toddlers to slide a British warship and a Turtle along its guided paths.

USS *ZUMWALT*

MANUFACTURER: Bath Iron Works **DATE OF PRODUCTION:** 2009–2013

There are many things you can do with $4 billion. One thing is to build a 610-foot-long, 17,535-ton (186-metre-long, 15,907-metric-ton) warship. A stealth warship, regarded as the most technologically sophisticated navy destroyer ever built! "If Batman had a warship, it would be the USS *Zumwalt*," says Navy Admiral Harry Harris. The Zumwalt has 80 bays for vertical missiles, two 155 mm Advanced Gun Systems that can hit targets 72 miles (116 kilometres) away, and two 30 mm rapid-fire guns for up-close protection. More impressively, the ship features an all-electric propulsion system. In fact, the ship can produce 78 megawatts of power—enough electricity to run a small city! Much of the electricity will likely be used for forthcoming high-energy weapons such as laser cannons. If this all sounds like science fiction to you, it'll come as no surprise that the ship's commander is Capt. James Kirk.

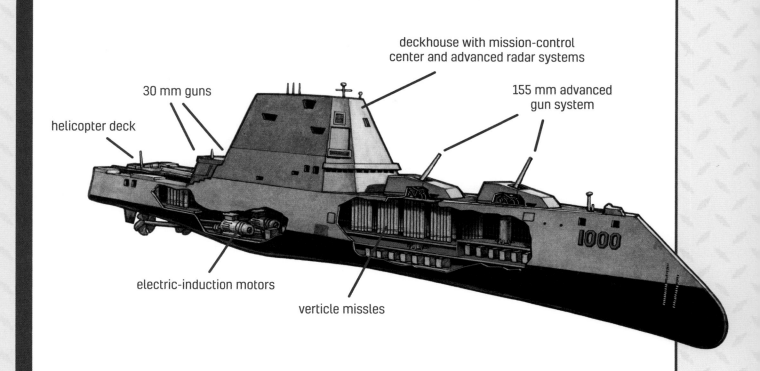

deckhouse with mission-control
center and advanced radar systems

30 mm guns

helicopter deck

155 mm advanced
gun system

electric-induction motors

verticle missles

1000

ZUMWALT. ZUMWAIT! ZUMWHAT?

The USS *Zumwalt* is the mother ship of the *Zumwalt* class of destroyers. The original plan was to build 32 *Zumwalts*, with a whopping budget of $22.5 billion. However, amazingly, that was not enough. So they reduced the quantity to just three *Zumwalts*.

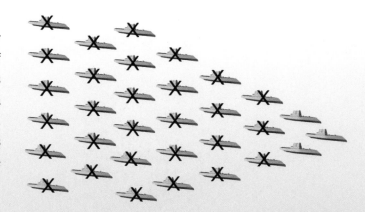

ZUMWHO?

The USS *Zumwalt* and other *Zumwalt*-class destroyers were named after naval officer Elmo Zumwalt Jr. (1920–2000). He was the youngest man to serve as the Chief of Naval Operations (i.e., the head of the U.S. Navy) and worked to end racial discrimination and provide a better life for sailors. Incidentally, his friends simply called him Bud.

VOYAGER

MANUFACTURER: The National Aeronautics and Space Administration (NASA) and the Jet Propulsion Laboratory (JPL)

DATE OF PRODUCTION: 1977

Over 40 years ago, two vehicles were launched into space—Voyager 1 and Voyager 2. The twin spacecrafts were sent to learn more about our solar system, to see if there was life out there, and to let aliens know that we are here. *Hello!*

Currently, Voyager 1 and 2 are more than 10 BILLION miles (16 BILLION kilometres) away from Earth, moving at speeds of over 35,000 miles (56,000 kilometres) per hour, leaving behind our solar system and entering the unexplored universe beyond!

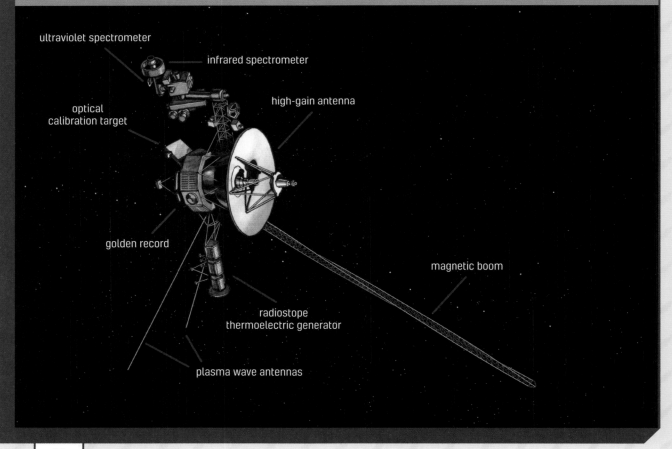

ultraviolet spectrometer

infrared spectrometer

optical calibration target

high-gain antenna

golden record

magnetic boom

radiostope thermoelectric generator

plasma wave antennas

Both Voyagers were launched into space just 16 days apart from each other onboard Titan Centaur rockets—Voyager 1 on September 5, 1977, and Voyager 2 on August 20, 1977.

THE GOLDEN RECORDS

Okay, they're really just gold-plated copper. But still! These phonograph records were included on both Voyager probes as a means of communicating with extraterrestrial life (that is, assuming extraterrestrials can figure out how to play a record). Good thing a stylus was included as well as basic instructions etched onto the aluminum cover. The album contains audio greetings in 55 languages, animal noises, the music of Beethoven, the sound of rain, and many other important things aliens might want to know about Earth.

DID YOU KNOW?

- The Voyager space probes are about the size of a midsize car, each with more than 65,000 parts.

- Voyager 1 took a picture for the first time of Earth and the moon together.

- The Voyager spacecraft were the first to see Jupiter, Uranus, and Neptune up close.

- Voyager 1 discovered erupting volcanoes on one of Jupiter's moons.

- Currently, the probes are so far away from Earth that it takes more than 15 hours for their radio signals (traveling at the speed of light) to reach us!

- The Voyager launches took place in 1977 as Jupiter, Saturn, Uranus, and Neptune were aligned in such a way that it was possible for the probes to visit each of the giant outer planets. The next outer planet lineup would not be for another 176 years.

- Both Voyagers will run out of power around the year 2025, at which point they will continue to drift among the stars until, maybe, just maybe, somebody or something finds them . . .

WALKING TRUCK

MANUFACTURER: General Electric   **DATE OF PRODUCTION:** 1965

"We Bring Good Things to Life," said General Electric. Whether or not the Walking Truck was a *good* thing is debatable. But it was definitely brought to life (our lives, that is) back in the 1960s. The Walking Truck was designed to help army infantry carry equipment over difficult terrain. A human operator sat in the middle of the vehicle and controlled each of the legs with a hydraulic system that followed the movement of her/his arms and legs. It was reported that "the strain of thinking about which leg to move next exhausted the operator after about 15 minutes and he had to take a rest." Yeesh. Still, at the time, it was considered "a landmark in the design of walking machines." And in fact, the mechanics were the predecessor to the robotic arms currently used by astronauts and doctors today. So there!

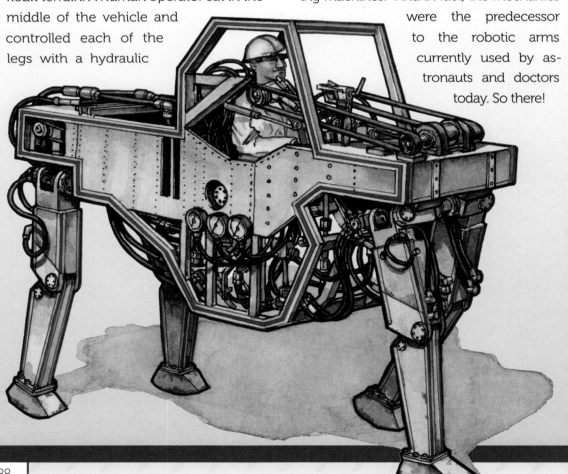

OLD-SCHOOL IRON MAN

Ralph Mosher, the Chief designer of the Walking Truck, also worked with General Electric to build the Hardiman—a mechanical exoskeleton that was supposed to allow the operator to lift loads of 1,500 pounds (680 kilograms). Unfortunately, the machine itself weighed close to 1,500 pounds (680 kilograms). Oops.

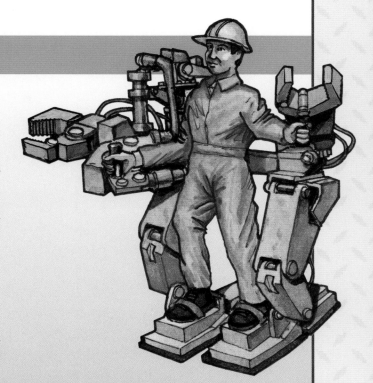

TRUE OR FALSE?

1. Other names for the Walking Truck include CAM (an acronym for Cybernetic Anthropomorphous Machine) and the Quadruped, which simply means "four-footed."

2. The Walking Truck was strong enough to push an entire jeep out of its way!

3. A major flaw of the Walking Truck was that it had to be attached to hydraulic power lines at all times and used 50 gallons (189 litres) of oil per minute!

4. Ralph Mosher was also commissioned by the Galactic Empire to design the AT-AT (or All-Terrain Armored Transport) for the Imperial Army.

5. The Walking Truck currently lives in the U.S. Army Transportation Museum in Fort Eustis, Virginia.

Answers: 1. True. 2. True. 3. True. 4. False. But maybe *Star Wars* director George Lucas was inspired by the Walking Truck. 5. True.

WINSTON WONG ICE VEHICLE

MANUFACTURER: Lotus Engineering   **DATE OF PRODUCTION:** 2010

Crossing Antarctica isn't easy. Having a Winston Wong Bio-Inspired Ice Vehicle certainly helps. Designed for the Moon-Regan Antarctic Expedition of 2010 (lead by Andrew Moon and Andrew Regan), this propeller-powered sled was driven across some seriously sketchy terrain: from the west coast of Antarctica to the South Pole, through the trans-Antarctic Mountains and down the Leverett Glacier. The team of ten took turns driving the WWBIIV while the other nine followed behind in two massive six-wheeled trucks, which contained monitoring equipment and were used as mobile laboratories. In total they traveled 2,485 miles (3,999 kilometres) over the course of 23 days. At times, the team was up against 60 mile (97 kilometre) per hour winds that created frozen windshields and severely limited visibility. Needless to say, this is less than ideal for traveling across a landscape that features hidden crevices and cliffs! The main objective of the journey was to monitor the environment as well as the environmental impact of the vehicles, but I sort of get the feeling that they really just wanted to travel across Antarctica in a Winston Wong Bio-Inspired Ice Vehicle!

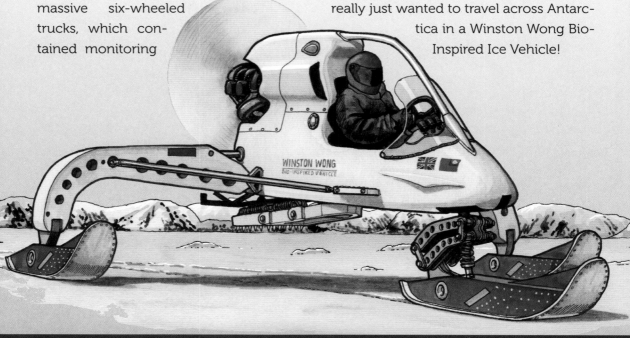

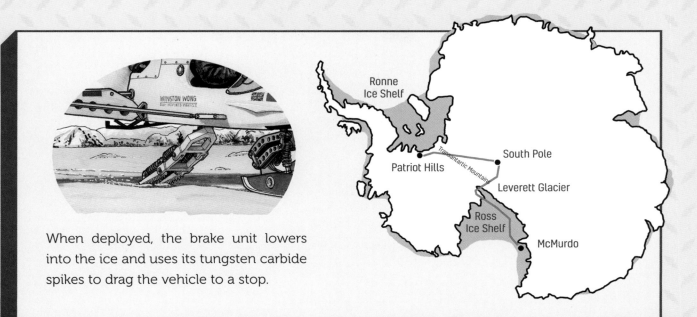

When deployed, the brake unit lowers into the ice and uses its tungsten carbide spikes to drag the vehicle to a stop.

WHICH ONE IS FALSE?

1. The 14.8-foot- (4.5-metre-) long ice vehicle runs off eco-friendly diesel.

2. The WWBIIV is 1,543 pounds (700 kilograms), which makes it light enough to be pulled by rope, should rope-pulling be needed.

3. The vehicle can travel at speeds of 84 miles (135 kilometres) per hour.

4. The driver can adjust the angle (or pitch) of the propellers' three blades, providing better fuel economy.

5. The driver of the vehicle is equipped with adjustable heat and a 5.1 surround-sound stereo system, allowing the driver to travel in subtropical warmth while rocking out to the Beach Boys.

Answer: Yup, it's #5. The vehicle has NO heat or stereo. In fact, the cabin is not even enclosed. Brrrrr.

WHO IN THE WORLD IS WINSTON WONG?

You mean you don't know? (It's okay, neither did I.) Winston Wong is a Taiwanese physicist, philanthropist, and entrepreneur. In partnership with Imperial College London, Dr. Wong funded the Moon-Regan Expedition, which of course included the Winston Wong Bio-Inspired Ice Vehicle. I wonder if the vehicle has a bumper sticker that says "WWWWD"?

ZAMBONI

MANUFACTURER: Zamboni **DATE OF PRODUCTION:** 1949–present

There are few words more fun to say than "Zamboni." Go ahead, try it! Turns out the Zamboni is also fun to watch as it zigzags back and forth across ice-skating rinks, cleaning and smoothing the surface of the ice. (Some might even say that the Zamboni is more fun to watch than whatever sport is taking place.) This machine has become an essential part of just about every ice rink around the world, as it quickly and efficiently shaves and skim-coats the surface, making a much smoother ride for hockey players, figure skaters, and those just trying not to fall.

HOW DOES IT WORK?

First, a sharp blade shaves a thin layer of ice from the surface.

Next, the machine sprays water onto the surface, cleaning out any remaining grooves. **Finally,** warm water is sprayed from the back of the machine, which in turn, is smoothed over by a heavy towel.

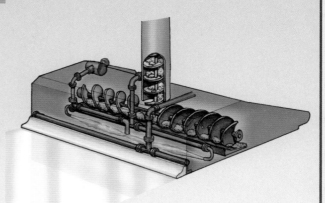

DID YOU KNOW?

The Zamboni Company (founded by Frank Zamboni) is not based in the icy mountains of Italy, or the hockey-obsessed countryside of Canada. Instead, its headquarters are in south Los Angeles, where the average temperature is 70 degrees Fahrenheit (21 degrees Celsius). The machines are tested by driving them through a palm-tree-lined neighborhood street to a local skating rink.

THE KLEENEX EFFECT

Just as all facial tissues are often referred to as Kleenex, the same holds true with ice-resurfacing machines. There are other brands out there, but none has as cool a name as Zamboni.

ZIL-2906

MANUFACTURER: Zil   DATE OF PRODUCTION: 1970

There's no shortage of Soviet-era unconventional vehicles. How about this screw-driven amphibious truck? As bizarre as it might seem, screw power can be quite effective, especially when trying to recover cosmonauts and space capsules from the middle of remote, swampy Siberia. The Zil-2906 (as well as the Zil-4904 and a few others) featured two large threaded cylinders on either side, which spun like giant corkscrews, pulling the 2-ton (1.8-metric-ton) vehicle across snow, ice, and even water. In addition, the cylinders were hollow, allowing them to act as floats! While it may not have been the speediest vehicle—10 miles (16 kilometres) per hour in water, 12 miles (19 kilometres) per hour in swamp, 28 miles (45 kilometres) per hour in snow—it certainly got to where it needed to go!

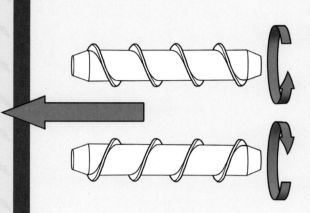

A BIT SCREWY

Screw-driven vehicles date back to 1899. Most, including the Zil-2906, move forward when the two screws rotate in opposite directions. In order to turn the vehicle, the screws rotate independently from one another. To move sideways like a crab, the screws spin in unison.

ZIL-4906

ZIL-2906

Soyuz capsule

ZIL TO ZIL

The Zil-2906 was specifically designed to recover Soyuz space capsules. To get to the recovery site, the 2906 would first be driven on the back of a six-wheeled Zil-4906 at speeds of up to 50 miles (80 kilometres) per hour. Once impassible terrain was reached, the Zil-4906 would use its onboard cranes to lower the 2906, allowing it to continue the journey.

между прочим (INCIDENTALLY)

"Zil" is short for "Zovad imeni Likhachova," which simply means "Likhachova Plant." This Moscow-based company also made some rather luxurious armored vehicles for government officials.

A CLOSING WORD OR TWO
(OR 270, TO BE EXACT).

Clearly, I like vehicles. When I moved to New York in 2001, however, I sold my van (a 1990 white Ford Aerostar I'd been using with my band), in large part because it was nearly impossible to find parking in Brooklyn. I have to say, it was one of the most invigorating things I've ever done. I discovered an amazing new form of transportation . . . walking! I was suddenly forced to get out and talk to people on the street, including some incredible neighbors who are some of my best friends today. I also met many great people at local restaurants and shops, one of which turned out to be the original headquarters for a book publisher. Over time, I developed a relationship with the staff at this store as well as a community of authors who worked with the publisher. And this, my friends, is a big part of why I started writing, and why you now have this book in your hands! Also, it felt really good to be one less person adding emissions to our overly polluted environment. Plus, how much fun is it to travel by subway? I realize not everyone is lucky enough to have a subway system, but I sure wish they did. Mass transit, carpooling, riding bikes, and, of course, walking are all important pieces of our future. And as they say, the future is now! Really, the point of this closing paragraph is just to say that vehicles are cool, but being considerate of the planet is even cooler.

P.S. And yes, the planet is definitely round (see page 59).

THANKS! THANKS A LOT!

First and foremost, a huge heartfelt thanks to the incredibly talented Hans Jenssen for working so hard on this book with me. You rock! Thank you, Jud Laghi, Melissa Manlove, Jay Marvel, Feather Flores, Abbie Goveia, Kevin Armstrong, Claire Fletcher, Jamie Real, Ariela Rudy Zaltzman, Marie Oishi, and everyone at Chronicle Books for making this entire series of books happen! Thanks to Kelly and Nathan for letting me sneak off to my studio so that I could research and write about human cannonballs and jet packs. Additional thanks to Charlie Atherton, Jason Bitner, Todd and Mason Clark, Richard Colacino and Regina Corallo, Olivier Conan and everyone at Barbès, Marshall Curry, Maggie Ford, Future Motion Inc., Ben Goldberg, Dan Graf, Tom Hatton, Hearsts, Grafs, and Eudaileys alike, Ben Holmes, Mike Howe, the Huffbunnies, Mike Hughes, Yonatan Israel and everyone at Colson Patisserie, Anders Johansson, Chip Jones, Amir Labidi, Allyssa Lamb, Saskia Lane, Steve Lewis, Emily Manzo, Juliane Marchi, Shawn Marren, Elizabeth Martin, Steve Mockus, John Murden, David Pescovitz, Nicki Pombier, Alan Rapp, Duke Riley, Leif Ristroph, Renee Slider, Stanford Solar Race Car Project, Dylan Thurston, Richie Trimble, Nicolai Voeckner, Don Walsh, Mel Ward, Margo Winton Parodi, Dean Wynton, Wyoming Territorial Prison State Historic Site, Dan Zanes, Carl Zucker, and all the kids (and grown-ups) who have been SO supportive of my career. I feel lucky and am extremely grateful. On a final note, I've written songs for every entry in this book. It's true! Visit me at www.michaelhearst.com.

Now go take a walk.

DEDICATED TO NATHAN, OF COURSE. —M. H.

Hey, check out SONGS FOR *UNCONVENTIONAL VEHICLES*.
There is a micro-tune for *each* entry in this book! Find the playlist at
michaelhearst.com

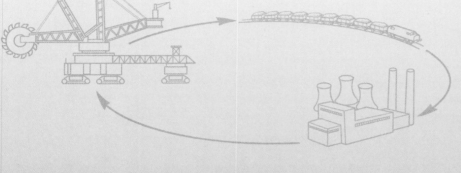

Text copyright © 2021 by Michael Hearst.
Illustrations copyright © 2021 by Hans Jenssen.

Library of Congress Cataloging-in-Publication Data available.

ISBN 978-1-4521-7286-6

Manufactured in China.

Design by Jay Marvel and Abbie Goveia.
Typeset in Museo.

10 9 8 7 6 5 4 3 2 1

Chronicle Books LLC
680 Second Street
San Francisco, California 94107

Chronicle Books—we see things differently.
Become part of our community at www.chroniclekids.com.